NOSTRADAMUS: PREDICTIONS OF WORLD WAR III

Jack Manuelian

Inner Light

First Edition: January 1995, by the author
under the title: *WWIII According to Nostradamus*
Revised Second Edition: 1996, by Inner Light Publications

PUBLISHED BY:
Inner Light Publications
Box 753
New Brunswick, NJ 08903
(free catalog on upon request)

Library of Congress Catalog Card Number: 94:096179
ISBN: 0-938294-52-0

"It is not the purpose here to describe conditions of doom or to arouse fear, rather to challenge and encourage. We should see these changes of earth as a time of labor, giving birth to a new age, to a 'new earth and new heaven.' Do not approach it in fear or with apprehension, but joyously."

Paul Solomon

• • • • • •

"And you will be hearing of wars and rumors of wars; see that you are not frightened, for those things must take place, but that is not yet the end."

JESUS CHRIST, (Matthew 24:6)

• • • • • •

"The changeover period between the Piscean and Aquarian Ages is an important one because it is the first time in recorded history that our species has had the ability to commit global genocide and to destroy the planet by either a nuclear holocaust or an ecological disaster."

Michael Howard

• • • • • •

"This star—your planet—was put in this universe and this galaxy for the purpose of becoming one of the great showcases or models of light. It is to be a major focal point or example of light, love and forgiveness for this entire galaxy.

"You are about to come out of darkness and blindness into light—into a stunning and incredible vision, (as a result of this photon belt experience, this great halo of change approaching our solar system and our world). Realize that what is going to happen is not something to fear. Rather, it is a gift of love, light, and grace leading to a great and glorious destiny for Earth's awakening prodigals."

The Sirian Council (To Sheldon Nidle)

ACKNOWLEDGMENTS

The author gratefully acknowledges permission to quote, or to take excerpts, from the following sources:

Newsletters: *Revelations of Awareness,* published by Cosmic Awareness Communications. *Rose Notes* and *Roses*, published by Our Lady of the Roses, Mary Help of Mothers Shrine. *The Earth Changes Report*, published by Matrix Institute, Inc.

Magazines: *TIME,* Time Inc.

Books: *Worlds in Collision* by Immanuel Velikovsky, Doubleday (a division of Bantam Doubleday Dell Publishing Group, Inc.). *Messages From God* by Dumitru Duduman, published by Hand of Help, Inc. *Conversations with Nostradamus,* Revised Edition, by Dolores Cannon, (Ozark Mountain Publishers:, Box 754, Huntsville, AR 72740, USA). *Behold A Pale Horse* by William Cooper, published by Light Technology/Intelligence Service. *You Are Becoming A Galactic Human* by Virginia Essence and Sheldon Nidle, published by Spiritual Education Endeavors Publishing Company.

Artworks: "Chick Publications" for its comic artworks. Jon Strongbow for his alien related artworks. "S.E.E. Publishing Co." for the photon belt and the figure of the Sirian artworks. The "Leading Edge Research Group" for the artwork of the underground laboratory.

The compilation and arrangement of the artworks and illustrations in this book are done by the author himself.

All scripture references are taken from the New American Standard Bible, © 1960–1977 by Lockman Foundation. Used by permission.

The author would like to thank the staff of the New York Public Library, in Manhattan, for their kind assistance while researching this work.

NOTICE: For more *COSMIC AWARENESS* information and a free sample newsletter, write: Cosmic Awareness Communications, P.O. Box 115, Olympia, Washington 98507, USA.

"A fascinating book on the next few years of crisis as predicted by Nostradamus…A visual and amusing book on such usually serious topics such as Armageddon, the Anti-Christ, the Papacy, Babylon, and WW III. UFO buffs will appreciate the last few chapters."

David H. Childress

• • • • • •

"Significant interpretation of Nostradamus' work that is well thought out and the author's interpretation has considerable validity in regard to his perception of Nostradamus. IT IS WORTH READING."

Cosmic Awareness

• • • • • •

"This book contain details about the origins and life of the legendary anti-christ. It is filled with illustrations to make the text clearer. This is a very interesting and worthwhile book."

OMEGA New Age Directory

• • • • • •

"With global conflicts shaping up as they are already this decade, the signs and scenarios given in the quatrains [of the book: *WW III ACCORDING TO NOSTRADAMUS*] now seem more realistic and plausible as the weeks go by. Indeed, if the love and awareness we bring to these times can affect our circumstances and surroundings for the better, then our fate as individuals and nations is by no means sealed."

NEXUS New Times Magazine

A Painting of Nostradamus by his son, Caesar

Contents

NOSTRADAMUS,

PAR

EUGÈNE BARESTE.

I. Vie de Nostradamus.
II. Histoire des Oracles et des Prophètes.
III. Centuries de Nostradamus.
IV. Explication des Quatrains prophétiques.

Orné d'un portrait authentique de Nostradamus,

PAR AIMÉ DE LEMUD.

DEUXIÈME ÉDITION.

Il est très-facile
de comprendre le goût
de tous les peuples pour les
livres prophétiques. Cette manie est le
résultat tout naturel du plus naturel de nos
penchants : l'amour du merveilleux et la curiosité.
Ce sont là certainement de très-grandes pauvretés de
l'esprit humain ; mais il est difficile de se défendre
de l'intérêt de curiosité qu'elles excitent
quand le hasard fait concourir la
prédiction d'un charlatan avec
l'histoire et, qui mieux
est, avec la vérité.

(CHARLES NODIER, *Mélanges tirés d'une petite bibliothèque.*)

PARIS.

MAILLET, ÉDITEUR, RUE DE L'EST, 31,
ET CHEZ TOUS LES MARCHANDS DE NOUVEAUTÉS.

1840.

The title page of Eugène Bareste's *Nostradamus*, 1840 second edition, Paris, from which the French quatrains in this book were taken after rendering the old French words to modern French spelling. Latin words have been left alone.

Introduction

TWO EXCERPTS FROM NOSTRADAMUS' EPISTLE TO HENRY II, THE KING

After this the barren dame [= Europe], of greater power than the second [Reich], will be received by two people.

—by the first [= Napoleon Bonaparte], who is made obstinate by God—

By the second [=Germans of Nazi Era and Hitler].

And by the third [= Turks or Arabs or Iranians] who will extend their forces towards the circuit of the East of Europe, into the Pannonians [the Balkans]—where they will be overwhelmed and slaughtered. And by sea they will make their extension into Sicily; into the Adriatic Sea through Macedonia; also extensions will be done toward Germany. They will succumb wholly and the Barbarian Sect will be greatly afflicted and driven out by the Latins.

Then the great Empire of the Antichrist will begin in the "Attila" and "Xerxes" [= Russia/China and Iran], and descend with great and countless numbers. Accordingly, the coming of the Holy Spirit proceeding from the 48th degree [= France] will make a transmigration, chasing out the abomination of the Antichrist: Making war against the Royal Pope, and upon the Church of Jesus Christ and His Kingdom.

Those events will be preceded by a solar eclipse more dark and gloomy than any since the creation of the world till the death and passion of Jesus Christ and it will be in the month of October that some great translation will be made, and it will be such that one would believe the mass of the planet has lost its natural movement and it is to be plunged into the abyss of perpetual darkness.

Before those events, there will be spring-like periods. But extreme changes will follow; reversals of realms [three great imperial powers were destroyed during WW I] and mighty earthquakes. These will be accompanied by the procreation of the new Babylon [= the Soviet Union], miserable daughter enlarged by the abomination of the first holocaust [= First World War]. It will last for only seventy-three years and seven months. [The Soviet Union/empire collapsed in 1991, after 73 years].

Then after, there will issue from the stock which had remained barren for so long, proceeding from the 50th degree [= from Poland] one [= Pope John Paul II] who will renew the whole Christian Church. A great peace will be established, with union and concord between some of the children of opposite ideas, who have been separated by diverse realms.

And the kingdom of the Rabid Ones [= West and East Germany], who would falsify sageness, will be united.

And the countries, towns, cities, realms and provinces which have left their first customs [of pre-Communist era] in order to achieve deliverance, but in reality they enthralled themselves still more [in the bondage of the Communist system], will secretly be displeased of their "liberty." And in order to regain their lost religion [of pre-Communist era], they will fall upon the party of the left, seeking a return to the right; and will put the so-long ignored holiness back into their old writings.

After the great dog [= Gorbachev], the biggest of curs [= Boris Yeltsin] will come, who will destroy all [the Communist system]; the same old crimes being perpetrated again . [Religious] temples will be set up again as in ancient times, and the PRIEST will be restored to his original position who will begin his whoring and luxury and will commit a thousands crimes.

[In order to recap:]

And being near to another desolation, by then she [the Soviet Union] will be at her most high and sublime dignity, potentates and military power/hands will be in rise [in Russia]; and they will take away his [= Gorbachev's] two swords [= his power], and to him will be left only the insignia, the bow, which will entice/inspire the people. The people will make him [= President Gorbachev] to go to the right and will not wish to submit themselves to those of the opposite extreme who likes to makes waves—up until there is born of a branch long sterile one [= Boris Yeltsin] who will deliver the whole people from this benevolent and voluntary slavery [of Communism]; he [= Yeltsin] will put himself under the protection of the military (Mars), discarding all honors and dignities—for the former freed [Soviet] empire, and will make his seat in a city located between two rivers [Moscow], and from which the chief [= Gorbachev] will be cast out and left jobless (hanging in the air), being in ignorance of the link of the conspirators with the new leader [= Yeltsin], a people's friend and lover of democracy (second Thrasibulus), who for a long time will have directed/plotted all this.

Then the impurities and abominations [of Communism], which were with great shame brought out and uncovered in the shadow of the reflecting light, will cease toward the end of the change of his [= Yeltsin's] reign.

And the leaders of the Church will be backward in the love of God and several will apostate from the true Faith. Of the three sects [= Judaism, Christianity and Islam] that which is in the middle [= Christianity], because of its own adherents, will be thrown a bit into decadence. The first one [= Judaism] will be exterminated totally in Europe and most of Africa by the third [= Islam] by means of those poor in spirit who, led by madmen to libidinous luxury, will adulterate [spiritually]. The [oriental Moslem] common people will rise up in support of extermination [of Jews] and chase out the adherents of the legislators [choosing despotism].

And it will seem that the way the nations are weakened by the Orientals that God the creator has loosed Satan out of his infernal prison in order to give birth to the great "Dog and Doham," [= a leader similar to the one known as "Gog and Magog" in the book of Revelation 20:7-9]. Those Orientals will make such an abominable fracture/schism in the Churches that neither the blind and helpless reds [= Cardinals] nor the whites will be in authority; their power having been taken away from them. So the churches will be persecuted in a way not seen up till then.

And during those events, a plague will be born that will be so great that more than two thirds of the people of the world will die. [Some indicate the word "plague" being a metaphor for Moslem invaders. However, this writer believe that a third disease, more deadly and more hideous than Aids and Ebola virus, will be introduced indirectly by aliens to speed up the destruction of the earth population]. So that fields and houses will stand empty and weeds will take over the streets of the cities. For the clergy there will be but utter desolation.

And the soldiers will usurp that which is being sent back from the City of the Sun [= Paris], from Malta and the islands of Hyères.

And the chains of the harbor of Marseilles will be opened. [also,3:79].

And a new incursion will be made by the maritime shores, wishing to deliver the Sierra Morena [in southern Spain] from the first Islamic recapture. Their assaults will not at all be in vain.

And the place which was once the habitation of Abraham [= Israel/Palestine] will be assaulted by persons who hold the Thursdays on veneration [= the followers of the third Anti-Christ]. And this city of Achen [= Jerusalem] will be surrounded and assailed on all sides by a most powerful of armed people. Their [= Israel's] maritime forces will be weakened from the western shores. And a great desolation will fall upon this realm, its greatest cities will be depopulated and those who enter within will fall under the vengeance of the wrath of God [because of contamination]. Oh, what a calamitous affliction will pregnant women bear at this time. [This ties in with Matthew 24:19 and Luke 21:23].

And it will come to pass then that because of the principal Oriental chief, the [world] will be stirred by the Northerners and Westerners; and most of the Orientals will be vanquished and put to death and overwhelmed and the rest will flee. [The surviving followers of the Oriental Arab chief] will be imprisoned.

[In order to recap] what great oppression will then fall upon those [vanquished] rulers of countries, specially the maritime and oriental ones, their tongues intermingled in a great society: the language of the Italians, and of the Arabs via north Africa. And all these Oriental rulers will be chased, overthrown and exterminated, not only by means of the forces of the Northern rulers, near the end of the age, [but] through three secretly united in pursuit of death and ambush, laying traps to one after the other. This renewed Triumvirate [U.S.A., Europe, Russia] will last for seven years, and the renown of this sect will extend throughout the universe. The sacrifice of the holy and immaculate host will be sustained. And it will be then that two Northern rulers will be victorious over the Orientals. They will make so great a noise and bellicose tumult that all the Orient will tremble of the fury of those two brothers [= allies], yet not Northern brothers.

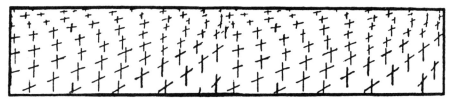

The wars of the Third Anti-Christ will transform southern Europe into a huge giant graveyard.

• • •

In the Epistle that some years ago I dedicated to my son, Cesar, I declared some points openly enough. But here, Sir, are included several great and marvelous events which those to come after will see.

And during this astrological calculations, in agreement with the sacred writings, the persecution of the Ecclesiastical people [= the Jews] will have its origin in the power of the Northern rulers [= the Nazis], united/allied with the Orientals [= the Japanese]. This persecution will last for eleven years [1933–44], or somewhat less, for then the chief Northern ruler [=Hitler], whose time being consummated, will fall.

It will happen unexpectedly that from its [= modern Israel's] southern united [part] will come one who will persecute even more violently the people of the Church for the space of three years through the Apostate seduction of one [= the third Anti-Christ] who will hold all the absolute power in the Church militant [= Islam]. The holy people of God, the observer of his law and ordinances of religion [= the Jewish people], will be greatly persecuted and afflicted, so much so that the blood of the true Ecclesiastics will flow everywhere.

One of the horrible temporal rulers will be praised by his followers for having spilt more human blood of the Innocent Ecclesiastics than anybody has done to wine. This ruler will commit incredible crimes against the Church. Human blood will run in public streets and churches, like the flow of water after an impetuous rain, coloring the nearby rivers red with blood. In another naval war, the sea will be reddened; so that a ruler's report to another would say: the waters have turned red because of naval battles.

Then in the same year and the following ones, there will ensue the most horrible and astonishing pestilence [= Moslem or Oriental invasion of Europe] because of the preceding famine, and such great tribulations the likes of which have not occurred since the Christian Church was first founded. It will cover all the latin regions, and will leave traces in some regions of Spain.

June 27, 1558

A nineteenth-century painting showing Nostradamus healing by the laying of the hand a sick child of King Henry II in 1564.

Chapter 1

THE PROPHET and HIS STYLE

• • • • • • • • • • • • • • • • • • •

The great seer of France, the greatest perhaps that the world has ever seen, was born Michel De Nostredame on December 14, 1503 in St. Remy, Provence. He was a devout Catholic, given to prayer, fasting and charity.

Although he was a renowned doctor of medicine by profession, in his later years he chose to become a seer, which brought him fame. Being a non-conformist and an unusual person by nature, he had to endure a great deal of opposition and ridicule. He once responded to a group of hecklers: "You will not make me swallow any of my words, neither in my lifetime, nor after my death." Even today, Nostradamus is an enigma to a vast majority of people and is reviled by many.

Nevertheless, he was a gifted man and was able to break the barriers of time. What he saw in the future made him tremble. He felt compelled to warn and prepare humanity in sufficient time so that the people and their leaders would change their actions and avert disaster.

He wrote some one thousand quatrains, as well as other prophetic literature hinting to what is in store for humankind. It was not his intention to play a puzzle game with his verses; living at the time of the Inquisition, he had no recourse but to be vague in order to protect himself from being executed and his writings being burned.

At sunrise on July 2, 1566, Nostradamus was found lying dead on the floor between his bed and a special bench which was built in order to maneuver his disabled body about the room.

His epitaph reads: "here rest the bones of the illustrious Michael Nostradamus, alone of all mortals judged worthy to record with his almost divine pen, under the influence of the stars, the future events of the entire world. He lived 62 years, 6 months and 17 days. He died at Salon in the year 1566. Let not posterity disturb his rest. Anne Pons Gemelle wishes her husband true happiness."

Nostradamus is now recognized as one of history's greatest prophets, due largely to the preciseness and accuracy of his prophecies, some of his quatrains refer to more than one event, doomed to happen in different time frames. Oftentimes, his quatrains have more than one meaning. Many of his verses are interconnected and they do have a sense of cyclic rhythm. Add to all this that he tried to include as much information in his writing - in a few words as possible - as he could, without making it clear whether he was speaking literally or figuratively. Thus, it is easy to understand why so many have complained about his crabbed and obscure style.

Moreover, Nostradamus deliberately confused the time sequences of his prophecies and did not use punctuation. He wanted to be on the safe side and avoid being persecuted by the powerful Catholic Church as a magician. Nostradamus remained a faithful Catholic and attended Mass regularly throughout his life. He apparently knew the Bible by heart and he relied heavily on scriptural concepts to get his point across.

A lesser known fact about Nostradamus is that he was also a professor of philosophy. Consquently his writings are full of abstract concepts. He loved to use symbolism, allegory, and analogy. He was fond of myths and mythology; he used the mythological idiom to convey thoughts which are beyond the realm of direct speech and straightforward language.

He referred to a country often by simply naming one of its cities. He veiled references to many places by the use of their ancient and historical names. Oftentimes, he used the names of cities or rivers to indicate a particular race. Names of famous classical characters are also used in his prophecies, like Nero for example, to indicate a modern bloody despot like Hitler (Century 9, Quatrain 53).

Nostradamus loved to play with words. He was an anagramist. Anagrams are words or phrases which are made by transposing the letters of other words or phrases. Letters of the word are scrambled to make another word, and sometimes letters are added or omitted from the new word. People in Nostradamus' time loved to play with anagrams, hence Nostradamus used anagrams liberally in his writings, especially when referring to proper names.

Some known anagrams of his are: "Chyrin" = Henry, "Pau.nay.loron" = Roy Napaulon = King Napoleon, "Hister" = Hitler, "Rapis" = Paris.

Nostradamus was an accomplished astrologer, ergo his writings are filled with astrological terms and expressions. Astrology was a respected science and practice in his day; learned men and professionals were expected to be versed in it. Nostradamus took full advantage of his expertise in Astrology. In his letter to his son, Caesar, he affirms that by "judicial astrology, together with divine inspiration and revelation, and continual nightly watches and calculations," that he has reduced his prophecies to writing. Further, he added, "thus, my son, you can easily understand that things which are to happen can be prophesied by the lights of the sky at night, which are natural, coupled with the spirit of prophecy." But Nostradamus was quick to emphasize that "the perfect knowledge of events cannot be acquired without divine inspiration, since all prophetic inspiration receives its prime motivating force from God the Creator rather than from fortune and nature."

Nostradamus' faith in God and his humble nature are made manifest in his Epistle to King Henry, where he did profess, "as for myself, I would never claim such a title [of a Biblical prophet], never, please God. I readily admit that all proceeds from God and render to Him thanks, honor and immortal praise. I have mixed therewith no divination coming from fate. All from God and nature, and for most part integrated with celestial movements."

Yet Nostradamus was great because he believed that "human affairs can be changed if enough people take control of their destiny and manage their day-to-day life fully informed of events and challenges facing them." Unfortunately, humans tend to be apathetic.

"Having been overtaken unexpectedly by [prophetic] ecstacy many times during a week; and having rendered my nocturnal studies pleasant by lengthy calculations, I have composed books of prophecies of which each contains one hundred astronomical quatrains of prophecies. I have sought to polish them a bit obscurely. They are perpetual prophecies, for they extend from now to the year 3799."

NOSTRADAMUS, first of March, 1555

Then God said, "Let there be lights in the expanse of the heavens to separate the day from the night, and let them be for signs, and for seasons, and for days and years" (Genesis 1:14).

In Medieval and Renaissance times, Astrology was under the blessing and sanction of God (and the Catholic Church), as it is shown in this engraving by Erhard Schön, c. 1515.

NOSTRADAMUS

Dieu se sert ici de sa bouche
Pour t'annoncer la vérité,
Si sa prédiction te touche
Rends grace a la Divinité.

Du livre de Guynaud.

An early source predicting WW III is a very extraordinary book of prophecy by the title *Liber Vaticinationem* written around 346 A.D. by an unknown seer. It has three quatrains in it about the three World Wars of our century (the third one yet to come):

For the first [WW] a noble is twice attacked
In the streets of ILLyria [in Yugoslavia] and dies.
The wolf [=Germany] lifts up its eyes to the moon [=moslem Turks].
And the Eastern empire [=czarist Russia] loses its head.

The "noble twice attacked" was the Austrian archduke Ferdinand whose assassination in Sarajevo on June 28, 1914, sparked WWI. There were two separate attempts to kill Ferdinand on that day.

In WWI the Germans and the Ottoman moslem Turks were allies. The crescent moon is a symbol of Islam.

During WW I the imperial Romanovs were destroyed by Communist takeover of Russia.

• • •

For the second [WW], Rome [of Mussolini] conspires with the wolf [=Germany]:
Between them they eat the [Roman] empire.
Mighty sounds lights up the nights,
And countless multitudes are trampled.

• • •

For the third [WW] the earth shakes.
The throat of the Gaul is ravaged.
Many die fleeing from the awful winds.
The sun halts in its path in the heaven.

In this quatrain "Gaul" is France. Historically, the Moslems are known to be fond of killing their enemies by slashing or splitting their throats; hence, a moslem invasion of France and Europe is implied.

Caesar, the son of Nostradamus

Nostradamus at the age of forty-seven.
(the year 1550)

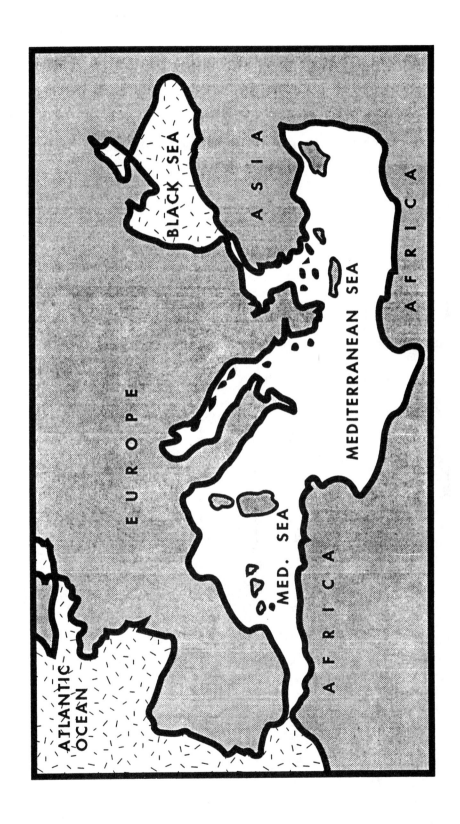

"Moreover, man does not know his times. Like fish caught in a treacherous net, and birds trapped in a snare, so the sons of men are ensnared at an evil time when it suddenly falls on them" (Ecclesiastes 9:12).

Chapter 2

PRELUDE To WORLD WAR III

• • • • • • • • • • • • • • • • •

Nostradamus wrote in his Epistle to Henry, King of France the Second, that most of his prophecies dealt with coming events which are to transpire in all of Europe, Africa, and part of Asia. He pointed to the period at the end of the second millennia and the beginning of the third millennia as being very critical.

He made predictions of regional wars occurring in the Middle East and the Mediterranean regions before the turn of this century.

First, a war is to break out between Greece and Turkey.

In his Epistle to the King, Nostradamus describes another war thusly: "The Third [Anti-Christ] will march his forces toward the circuit East of Europe, at Lower and Upper Pannonia [modern Yugoslavia and Hungary], where he is defeated; and by sea he will reach Trinacria [Sicily], and by the way of Myrmidons [Macedonia] into the Adriatic and Germany. He will be defeated from all, and the Barbarian sect will be greatly afflicted and driven out from among the Latins [the Italians]."

The "Third" in the preceding quotation is the Anti-Christ from the Middle East who will launch a campaign against Italy and the Balkans. He will be defeated and thus fail in his first attempt to conquer Europe.

According to Nostradamus, at the beginning of the Twenty First Century, the world will be fast approaching World War III. He made the following statement in his Epistle: "The events which will take place at the beginning of the seventh millennia [that is the third millennia A.D.], when, so far as my profound astronomical circulations and other knowledge have been able to make out, the adversaries of Jesus Christ and His Church will begin to multiply greatly."

Farther in the same Epistle a new war is portrayed; the armies of three allies, namely that of the Arab Anti-Christ, of Iran (Xerxes) and of Russia/Central Asia (Attila), all will join forces and invade Europe. Nostradamus wrote, "Then the great Empire of the Anti-Christ will begin in 'Attila' and 'Xerxes' and come down with great and countless numbers, so that the coming of the Holy Ghost, proceeding from the 48th degree [France?], will transmigrate, chasing out the abomination of the Anti-Christ, who made war against the Royal who is the great Vicar of Jesus Christ, and against his Church, and whose reign will be for a time and to the end of time."

However, just before the defeat and destruction of the Arab Anti-Christ, whose second campaign will last for 27 years, Nostradamus predicted/specified a "solar eclipse more dark and gloomy than any since the creation of the world, except that after the death and passion of Jesus Christ. And it will be in the month of October that some great dislocation [shifting of the poles?] will transpire and it will be such that one will think the mass of the earth has lost its natural movement and that it is to be plunged into the abyss of perpetual darkness."

As for the end of the third millennia, Nostradamus predicts another universal conflagration. His quatrain No. 74, from the century No. 10 states:

At the completion of the great seventh number,
And at the time of the slaughter games,
- Not far from the great age of the millennium -
It will appear that the dead have risen from their graves.

The great seventh number is the seventh millennium reckoned from the creation of Adam; it corresponds to the third millennium if reckoned from the birth of Christ. **A time of slaughter games** is a time of global warfare. **The dead rising from the graves** signifies the coming of the judgment day, as many will die leaving their bodies behind.

In his letter to his son, Caesar, Nostradamus writes: "As to visible heavenly judgment, when we (that is mankind) are at the seventh millennia number which completes all, we will be approaching the eighth sphere, where is located the firmament of the eighth sphere, in latitudinal dimension, where the great eternal God will come to complete the revolution, where the heavenly bodies will return to their movement, and the superior movement [orbit?] will render the earth stable and firm - not inclining from age to age, unless God wills it otherwise."

TURKEY: A WOULD BE HOT SPOT

The post-cold-war Turkey has a much bigger regional agenda; it is at the center of its own geo-political world. It has interest in central Asia with Turkish population there, in the Caucasus with Turkish populations and a deep interest in the Balkans as well.

"Pan-Turkism represents a significant danger for Iran. A successful Turkish penetration into Central Asia does not serve China's interests. The Russians hate the Turks and vice versa. Without access to warm waters, it is difficult for Russia to remain a super power. Even if she has to resort to extreme measures, Russia will not permit Turkey to make the necessary inroads into Central Asia or within the former Soviet Union."

Turkey's Southeastern Anatolia project is a plan that centers on 22 dams and 19 power plants in the Tigris-Euphrates basin. After Turkey built the Ataturk-Dam to contain Euphrates river, both Syria and Iraq have complained of shortages of water and power. Sooner or later, Syria and Iraq have to wage war against Turkey, solely over water.

Greece and Turkey have long disputed control over the Aegean Sea. Under the international Law of the Sea Convention, which took effect Nov. 16, 1994, Greece has claimed the right to extend its control 12 miles. Turkey has threatened to go to war to prevent the extension of Greece's territorial waters.

This wouldn't be just an Aegean war; it would be a larger Balkan war, potentially with Moslem versus anti-Moslem forces, and could well involve forces from Russia.

On June 1, 1995, the Greek Parliament ratified the international Law of the Sea treaty. Turkey has refused to sign the treaty. The ratification gives Athens the right to double its territorial waters, to 12 nautical miles from shore. Greece said it will exercise its rights whenever its interests dictate. Turkey said any move to do so would be a warlike act.

Turkey argues that the enforcement of the treaty would bring all Aegean shipping, as well as fishing and mineral rights, under Greek control.

If Greece forcibly extend its control, then the potential for an Aegean war (to ignite a regional conflict that could well involve forces from Russia, Iran and the Balkans) would become a real danger.

Actually, the true rulers in Turkey are the military men retired or in uniform; mostly from rural areas, they basically are nationalist, fundamentalist and racist.

On May, 1995, Thomas Freidman wrote in *N.Y. Times*: "Turkey today provides one-stop shopping to all the troubles of the post-cold-war world. Turkey is connected geographically, ethnically or politically to the problems of Iraq, Iran, Armenia, Azerbaijan, Bosnia, Cyprus,

Greece, Bulgaria, Russia, Tajikistan, Syria and Islamic fundamentalism [Islam is on rise again in Turkey]. All the Turks are missing is a border with Chechnya."

A WAR BETWEEN GREECE AND TURKEY

Century 1, Quatrain 83: "La gent étrange divisera butins/Saturne en en Mars son regard furieux/Horrible strange aux Toscans et Latins/ Grec, qui seront à frapper curieux.

TRANSLATION:
The alien nation will divide the spoils.
Saturn In Mars its aspect furious.
The horrible slaughter will astonish the Tuscans and Latins.
The Greeks will be provoked to strike.

The **alien nation** is Turkey. The Turks are strangers and aliens to the Middle East. In the Middle Ages, waves of predatory Turkish tribes from the steppes of central Asia marched westward and conquered Arab and Christian kingdoms in the East and West. They called the Armenian and Byzantine lands in Asia Minor their own; and set out from there to conquer Europe.

The Greeks are historical enemies of the Turks. In the forthcoming war they will be tricked by the Turks to open fire first. The war will not last long because the Turks will resort to the use of chemical, biological and tactical nuclear weapons. The resulting horrible slaughter will keep the Italians from interfering and coming to the help of Greece.

The **spoils** are the Greek islands in the Aegean Sea. They have been coveted by the Turks ever since their conquest of Asia Minor.

Saturn is the archetypal taskmaster among the planets. Most of the other planets reveal their problematical side when combined with Saturn. The planet **Mars** symbolizes the god of war; Mars' influence brings conflict and destruction.

A BURNING HEAT IN GREECE

C.2, Q.3: "Pour la chaleur solaire sus la mer/De Negrepont les poissons demis cuits/Les habitans les viendront entamer/Quand Rod. et Gennes leur faudra le biscuit."

Because of the solar heat upon the sea,
At Negropont the fishes will be half cooked.
The inhabitants will come to dress and eat them,
While in Rhodes and Genoa the crop will fail.

Negropont is an ancient name for Euboea, one of the largest islands of Greece in the Aegean Sea. Its main city is Negropont or modern Khalkis, an important city as early as the 7th century B.C., and an invasion point for campaigns against Greece.

Rhodes is another big Greek island in the south-east Aegean Sea. **Genoa** is a maritime city in Italy.

This quatrain refers to a great heat from the sun that will cause the fishes to die from extensive heat, while there will be famine in the land because of crop failure due to the heat wave.

It is amazing how a prophecy given by Saint Theresa to Veronica Lueken, the Bayside seer of New York, almost parallels the prediction of Nostradamus. The second part of Saint Theresa's poem, given in 1981, reads:

The heat of the sun will burn skin from the bones;
Then shed no light to brighten dark homes.
The moon will be covered in morning haze;
Then give off a red cast in solid maze.
The seas will be empty, the ground found bare;
There will not be food for any to share.
Then many shall gnash their teeth in woe;
For now they have watched the seeds they did sow.

WAR AND DEVASTATION IN GREECE

9:91 "L'horrible peste, Perynthe et Nicopplle,/Le Chersonne tiendra et Marceloine,/La Thessalie vastera l'Amphipolle,/Mal inconnu et le refus d'Antoine."

**A horrible pestilence will fall upon Corinth, Nicopolis, and
The Gallipoli Peninsula. It will devastate Macedonia and
Thessaly. In Amphipolos
An unknown evil, and the refusal of Antony.**

Antony in line four refers to Mark Antony (Marcus Antonious, c82-30 BC), the Roman general who became one of the three joint rulers of the Roman empire with his brother-in-law Octavian and Lepidus. Antony controlled the east from the Adriatic to the Euphrates, but alienated Octavian by falling in love with the Egyptian queen, Cleopatra and combining forces with her. Attacked by Octavian, Antony, rather than giving up and surrendering, committed suicide after his naval defeat at Actium.

This quatrain implies that Greece will refuse to surrender to the enemy, and consequently will be destroyed by chemical, biological, and nuclear weapons.

"BORISTHENES" WILL COME TO FAIL

3:95 "La loy moricque on verra défaillir/Après une autre beaucoup plus séductive/Boristhenes premier viendra faillir/Par dons et langue une plus attractive."

**The law of More will be seen to fail,
For another much more seductive.
Boristhenes first will come to fail,
By gifts and tongues to another more attractive.**

The **law of More** refers to the Socialism/Communism of Sir Thomas More which found fertile ground in Russia. Nostradamus correctly predicted its failure. Line two refers to the present resurgence of the Russian imperialist and nationalist movement.

Boristhenes or Boryshtenes is an ancient name for the river Dnieper in Russia. Nostradamus used it as an anagram for Boris Yeltsin, indicating Russia in the same time.

Borisithenes = Boris-then-es = Boris Esthen = Boris Yeltsin.

The first line has also been interpreted as referring to the Moors who are north African people of mixed Berber and Arabic stock, living in Algeria, Morocco, Tunisia and Libya. In December 1991, the Islamic militants began their insurgency in Algeria after the Islamic Salvation Front swept the initial round of first free parliamentary elections. When the military in Algeria banned the Front and cracked down on its supporters, the Fundamentalists responded with a campaign of terror and violence that has claimed nearly 40,000 lives, arousing fears of a full-fledged civil war dangerously spreading to the whole of North Africa.

Hence, in this quatrain, Nostradamus is predicting first the downfall of B. Yeltsin in Russia, followed by a successful Islamic militant takeover in north Africa.

THE WOLF AND THE BEAR TO DEFY EACH OTHER

5:4 "Le gros mâtin de cite dechassé/Sera fâché de l'étrange alliance/ Après aux champs avoir le cerf chassé/Le loup et l'ours se donront défiance.

The gross mastiff is driven out of the city,
He will be vexed by the strange alliance.
After having chased the deer to the fields,
The wolf and the bear will defy each other.

The **gross mastiff** is Boris Yeltsin. The **city** is Kremlin. The strange alliance vexing Mr. Yeltsin is the nationalist and communist powers in the new Russian parliament.

To **chase the deer to the fields** means that Russia will become belligerent, while the deer symbolizes meekness and peacefulness.

The **wolf** in line four refers to the West, and the **bear** refers to Russia in her role as a new world power.

A trance reading or interpretation by Paul Shockly about Vladimir Zhirinovsky, given in early January 1994, indicates that (what follows is a condensation of that reading. For the whole reading ask for the newsletter REVELATIONS OF AWARENESS No. 430, 1994–4, from: Box 115, Olympia, WA 98507, USA): "There is a great intensity motivating this entity [Zhirinovsky] in such a way as to make him potentially dangerous to many people of the world, and giving great hope to certain people of the world also. The entity is extremely controversial and his activities could indeed lead the world into a third world war. The entity is one who could easily become a modern dictator. This Awareness indicates indeed, although it appears that Yeltzin will continue being in charge for some time yet, it appears that indeed Zhirinovsky is a great threat to Yeltzin's control of Russia and that with continued effort on his part, he may well be in charge of that nation within a short time, perhaps within two or three years or even sooner. But as he grows in power, if he gains the power he seeks, he will be indeed a great force for good or ill in the world. This Awareness indicates it is likened unto thinking that Russia is now disarmed and harmless and out of a kind of blatant hostility, leaving her alone to suffer from her own demise, while not realizing that there is a time-bomb in the midst of that country which is ticking away and which might explode into a new kind of revolution wherein the country suddenly revives into a different creation to become a new threat to the world. This Awareness indicates that **It** did not imply that the entity [Zhirinovsky] was a demagogue, but it is clear that the entity is capable of being such. It is also possible the entity could act in such a way as to bring on a third world war which is not something entities [people] will desire. Thus the entity [Zhirinovsky] for good or ill, as a force on the scene today, needs to be reckoned with, needs to be understood and the influences that act upon him from the rest of the world, particularly from the powers of the Western world, are going to help determine what this entity's future is in terms of his effect on the rest of the world. This Awareness indicates the entity could fade away as quickly as he appeared on the scene, or the entity could rise to greater heights of fame or notoriety. The future is not fixed in regard to this entity. He is not what entities might think of as the antichrist, nor is he a savior of mankind, but he is capable of moving toward either of these extremes, and it is likely that he will rise to greater heights of power before he makes a choice as to which position or direction he moves in regard to the relations with the New World Order. This Awareness indicates that the super-powers [i.e. super economical powers - the Rothschilds and Rockefellers and so forth] of the West are certainly doing a great deal of investigating and research into this entity's background and his personnel behavior and values to determine whether they can control him, work with him, or whether they should, for their own sake, find ways to destroy him. This Awareness indicates that whatever their choice is, their behavior toward him is going to affect his reaction to the Western world, and to his own position in his native land. It is not yet clear as to his destiny in the face of humanity. This Awareness indicates that at this stage, the entity [Zhirinovsky] appears to be in opposition to the Western world and the super-powers; by super-powers this Awareness refers to super economic powers: the Rothschilds and Rockefellers and so forth. The entity's opposition to these powers will give him a degree of strong support from his countrymen at a time when Russia feels weakened and incapable of attending to her own needs. People will look at this man and see him as a strong leader who could take them out of their present morass and lead them to become a new world power."

THE WEST IS TO EXPERIENCE VIOLENT CHANGES

1:55 "Sous l'opposite climate Babylonique/Grande sera de sang effusion/Que terre et mer, air, ciel sera inique/sects, faim, regne, peste, confusion."

In the opposite climate than of Babylon,
The effusion of blood will be great.
The atmosphere and heaven will be unfair to the earth and sea.
Sects, famine, plagues, and confusion will predominate.

The **opposite of the tyrannical Babylon** is the democratic and the free countries of the West where violence and shedding of blood will soon be great. Nature will be in turmoil, out of control. The political parties (**sects**) will rise and fall, and the coming changes will confuse the people.

EUROPE IS IN TURMOIL

2:39 "Un an devant le conflit Italique/Germain, Gailois, Hespagnols pour le fort/Cherra l'école maison de république/Ou, hors mis peu, seront suffoqués morts."

A year before the Italian conflict,
The Germans, the French, and the Spanish are in darkness.
The republican school house is closed,
Where, except for the few, the rest will suffocate to death.

The French phrase **pour le fort**, when in the masculine form, could mean "to be on the defensive or in heat" or it could mean "to be on the side of the strong." It also signifies "to be in the thickest part of a forest," in other words, to be in darkness. Hence, the Germans, the French, and the Spaniards are going to be in political darkness one year before the war (**conflict**) in Italy.

Free speech is going to be prohibited, and teaching in schools controlled. Most people will suffer in the suffocating darkness of repression.

A CIVIL AND A RELIGIOUS WAR IN ITALY

7:8 "Flora, fuis, fuis le plus proche Romain/Au Fesulan sera conflict donné/Sang espandu les plus grands prins à main/Temple ne sexe ne sera pardonné."

Flora, flee, flee from the near kinsman of the Roman.
At Fiesole the battle will be given.
Blood is to be shed; the great ones are to be shackled,
Neither temple nor sex will be spared.

It is apparent from this quatrain that the Catholic Church will be divided and a civil and religious war will ensue, with much bloodshed and many leaders made captive.

Flora is the goddess of flowers, gardens, and love in mythology. She married Zephyrus and received from him the gift of enjoying perpetual youth. Nostradamus' request is that those who cherish life, love, and flowers, let them flee the "near kinsman of the Roman," an apparent reference to a strong religious character. **Temple and sex** that are not going to be spared refer to nuns, monks, and priests.

Fiesole or ancient Faesulae, is a town in central Italy, four miles northeast Florence. Most likely, Nostradamus mentioned it as a reference to Italy.

A WORSENING "STORM" TO HIT ITALY

2:15 "Un peu devant monarque trucidé/Castor Pollux en nef, astre crinite/L'erain publique par terre et mer vide/Pise, Ast, Ferrare, Turin, terre inderdite."

Shortly before the monarch is killed,
Castor and Pollux are in the ship. One star is bearded.
The public fund is spent over sea and land.
Pisa, Asti, Ferrara, and Turin are forbidden lands.

The **monarch** in this quatrain refers to the pope; either to John Paul II or to his successor, known as the "Olive Tree" pope.

Castor and Pollux are twin brothers in mythology. When sailing at sea they were hit by a storm. Two stars appeared over their heads and the storm miraculously ended. So the legend has it that during storms at sea, if two lights are seen at the top of ship's masts, the storm will cease. If only one light appears, then the storm will grow worse. At times, the term "bearded star" is used in astronomy to describe comets.

Apparently Italy will be facing the clouds of war, and consequently will be forced to spend her public fund for defenses of her lands and waters.

Due to the effects of the war, the area by the Italian towns Pisa, Asti, Ferrara, and Turin are going to be forbidden zones. The above mentioned towns or communes are located in the west and northwest of Italy.

A DROUGHT IN ITALY AND A MILITARY INTERVENTION IN BOSNIA

2:84 "Entre Campaigne, Sienne, Flora, Tuscie/Six mois neuf jours ne plauvra une goutte/L'étrange langue en terre Dalmatie/Courira sus, vastant la terre toute."

Between Campania, Siena, Florence, and Tuscany,
It will not rain a drop for six months and nine days.
The strange language in the land of Dalmatia
Will run throughout, devastating the whole earth.

Campania is an exceedingly fertile region of central Italy, south of Rome, whose principle city is Naples. **Tuscany** is a region west central, north of Rome. It is mostly mountainous, with fertile river valleys and coastal areas. It has many famous cities such as Florence, Siena, and Pisa.

Dalmatia is a region in Croatia consisting of a mountainous strip bordering the Ardiatic. It extends from near the Albanian border on the south to Zara or Zadar on the north and includes about 300 islands.

The **strange language** in Dalmatia refers to a military intervention in all of that area, engulfing the whole earth in global warfare.

THE SPECTER OF FAMINE IN ITALY

3:42 "L'enfant naîtra à deux dents en la gorge/Pierre en Tuscie par pluie tomberont/Peu d'ans après ne sera blé, ni orge/Pour saouler ceux qui de faim failliront."

The child will be born with two teeth in his mouth,
It will rain stones in Tuscany.
A few years after there will be neither wheat nor barley,
To feed those who would be dying from hunger.

The first line is allusion to new born babies eating solid food (**born with two teeth**) because of lack of milk.

There is famine in the land, as the fertile farmlands of Tuscany will not be receiving any rain (**will rain stones**).

A HORRIBLE DEVASTATION AFTER THE DEATH OF MABUS

2:62 "Mabus puis tôt alors mourra, viendra/De gens et bêtes une horrible défaite/Puis tout à coup la vengeance on verra/Cent main, souf, faim, quand courra la comète."

Mabus then shortly will die, there will come
A horrible devastation of people and animals.
Then suddenly the vengeance will be seen
When the comet shall pass. Hundred hands, thirst and hunger.

Mabus is most likely an anagram for "Musa" = Moses. The first line could be an allusion to the death of the penultimate pope, referred to as the "Olive Branch or Tree" by Nostradamus. In sextet No. 30, Nostradamus predicts his death by being poisoned, though it will appear to the public that he died from fever.

Mabus could also indicate an Iranian patriot who will overthrow the rule of the Ayatollahs in Iran. Unfortunately, this modern Megabyzus (or MABUS for short) will be assassinated soon afterwards.

The **vengeance** in line three refers to the wrath or judgment of God upon a godless and unrepenting humanity. It will descend in the form of a killer comet passing close to earth or actually hitting our Globe. Thereupon, wide-spread thirst and hunger will follow for 500 days (100 hand x 5 fingers in each hand = 500).

It is amazing how several warnings about a comet striking the earth (just after World War III commences) were given to Veronica Lueken, the seer of Bayside, from Heaven. On July 25, 1973 Veronica described that great calamity as Mother Mary showed her in a vivid vision thusly: "I see a large globe suspended in the air; it is the globe of the earth. I see this large ball [comet], it's heading very fast, with its long tail behind it giving off these gases. It's very big, and it's very long, and way off in the distance, I can see what is a ball [a comet] it's like a sun, very burning and red. It seems to be going all around the sun as though it's being pulled in. But no, now the ball [the comet] is beginning to turn; it's bouncing.

"And now the ball is making a dive into....the path of the earth. Now it's caught like a top, and it's spinning. And it's starting to....[revolve] around, around the earth, and the tail now is pulling away from the sun. And the ball is going around the earth, and the tail now is starting to drift over onto the earth. I see now the oceans, the waters. I see the waters churning up, and this land [USA] is just going down into the water. Oh-h!"

On December 24, 1973 another vision of the same comet was given to Veronica from Heaven: "Oh! I see the sky, it's becoming a very, very bright red, almost an orange, a red-orange, and the light is so bright it hurts my eyes. And I see this huge gray colored ball, a rock-like formation, as it's turning now, it's changing color, becoming an orange-looking ball. And it's going fast across the sky, part of it has broken off, and it's going now behind the sun. I see the huge sun; it's a ball of fire. And this [comet] is another ball of fire. And a piece now is broken off, and it's hitting into the sun. And oh! there is an explosion! I can't look. Oh-h-h! And I see people now holding onto the chairs in their houses. Everything's rocking; the very foundation is rocking in the houses. And they are all frightened. And many are running into the streets, others are running and closing their windows. I see a great mist coming in the sky, and there are pieces of dust rock falling. And the people who are outside are stumbling. And I see now this darkness - a great, great mist. And then a deep, musty-looking haze, and it's now going and passing across the moon. And now there's no moon; there's no light. The moon's absolutely covered. I can't see it; there's no light. Now the sun also seems to be shooting out particles, and I can see this other ball [the comet] that looks like a small sun now, coming from behind, twirling and also shooting out particles of fiery rock. Now one piece is very large, and it's falling down, it's falling into the water, and the water is rising very, very high. Oh!"

On July 25, 1985 Veronica once again viewed the horror of the comet: "I see a ball of fire [the comet]; it's coming fast through the sky, it has a long red tail. It's red, it's fire! And now it's coming down to the earth. Oh! It has hit through the water; it's brushed through the water. There are waves rising higher, higher than anything possible I could have seen. The waves are terrible. They're washing half of the continent [of America] out to sea."

Apparently, an human attempt to blow-up the comet in the sky, in order to render it harmless, would fail. On December 24, 1973 Veronica had the following vision: "I can see that great ball [the comet] again. It's very, very large. Oh, my goodness! And now there's also something over to the left of the ball. It looks like a space-ship or something long with casing. And I see that it's behind it, but all of a sudden I see the top of this metal casing blow off; like disintegrating from the intense heat of this large ball [the comet]. Oh, my goodness! (Veronica coughs) The smoke! Oh, my goodness! Oh, I see now there are people inside of this metal-like casing starting to explode. And it just blew into a million pieces and there's nothing left of it. I can't see anything; it just seemed to explode and be carried away by a great force. There's not a thing left of it. Oh!"

On July 25, 1977 Jesus said in a vision through Veronica: "My children, much of the sorrow that will be sent upon mankind, much of it will come about because of his own making. The greatest loss of life, My children, will come with the explosion of a nuclear warhead upon mankind. The ball of Redemption shall follow, and not much shall be left of flesh upon earth."

On June 18, 1991, Jesus gave the following warning through Veronica: "My child and My children, you will keep a constant vigilance of prayer going throughout your world, because, I repeat again, near the throne of the eternal Father, He views a ball so immense, so beyond all man's speculation, that it will destroy over three-quarters of the earth. It is in your atmosphere. It has been noticed by few, but the few seek not to bring fear to the hearts of mankind. They do not know that it is the Eternal Father who now will guide that Ball."

On September 6, 1976, Mother Mary told Veronica: "Pray that mankind will awaken and escape this great Chastisement, My child. It will rush into your atmosphere without warning. Scientists will look with fright, as will the ordinary man. Know, my child, that no scientist will know an explanation for its appearance."

On June 18, 1988 Mother Mary affirmed to Veronica and to the faithful gathered at Our Lady of the Roses, Mary Help of Mothers Shrine prayer vigil held at the Vatican Pavilion site in Flushing, New York: "Within this century this Ball [the comet] will be sent upon mankind....It will be here within this century [before year 2000]. For even the scientists have failed to recognize the speed of this ball."

On July 1994 when asked astronomer Carolyn Shoemaker about a comet, such as Shoemaker-Levy heading our way, toward earth, about the warning time we will get on that she answered: "If it was a comet that we know of ahead of time, a periodic comet on a fairly low orbit, we would know about it perhaps ten years ahead, by the time it approached lot closer we would know rather precisely where it might impact. *But if a comet should appear from behind the sun. we might only have a one or two year warning.*"

Immanuel Velikovsky indicates in his book, **Worlds in Collision** (1950), that about "fifty comets move between the sun and the orbit of Jupiter; their periods are under nine years....and that, besides the comets of short periods, several hundred thousand comets visit the solar system....They are seen presently at an approximate rate of five hundred in a century....every comet has its peculiar shape which may also change during the visibility of the comet."

In the same book, Velikovsky explains what may happen when a planet has a close encounter with a comet: "A planet turns and revolves on a quite circular orbit around a greater body, the sun; it makes contact with another body, a comet, that travels on a stretched out ellipse. The planet slips from its axis, runs in disorder off its orbit, wanders rather erratically, and in the end is freed from the embrace of the comet. The body on the long ellipse experiences similar disturbances. Drawn off its path, it glides to some new orbit; its long train of gaseous substances and stones is torn away by the sun or by the planet, or runs away and revolves as a smaller comet along its own ellipse; a part of the tail is retained by the planet comet on its new orbit."

Velikovsky also mentions that "a comet with a head as large as the earth [a great ball of a comet], passing sufficiently close, would raise the waters of the oceans miles high."

Velikovsky also discloses in his book that "a comet, encountering a planet, can become entangled and drawn away from its own path, forced into a new course, and finally liberated from the influence of the planet is proved by the case of Lexeil's comet, which in 1767 was captured by Jupiter and its moons. Not until 1779 did it free itself from this entanglement."

Recently, James Reston Jr., in an article in TIME (May, 23, 1994), said: "if such a comet train [the Shoemaker-Levy] hit one of Earth's oceans, tidal waves would deluge and destroy the closest coastlines. If it hit land, it could incinerate whole countries and kick up a cloud of dust that would blot out the sun and bring on a nuclear winter. Millions, perhaps billions, of people would die."

TURKEY AND EGYPT ARE INVADED

5:25 "Le prince Arabe, Mars, Sol, Venus, Lyon/Regne d'Eglise par mer succombera/Devers la Perse bien près d'un million/Bisance, Egypte ver. serp. invadera."

The Arab prince: Mars, Sun, Venus, Leo.
The kingdom of the Church will succumb by the sea.
Toward Persia a sizable army of a million.
"Versus Serpens" will invade Byzantium and Egypt.

In the first line Nostradamus portrays the Arab Anti-Christ through the astrological terms of Mars, Sun, Venus, Leo. He presents to us a person in his prime, aggressive, ambitious, pushy, temperamental and egotistical. This independent person with leadership abilities will turn out to be a dictatorial and authoritative ruler full of pride. He will succeed in breaking down the Catholic Church by an attack from the sea.

The prophet Daniel describes the same person more directly: "A king will arise insolent and skilled in intrigue. And his power will be mighty, but not by his power, and he will destroy to an extraordinary degree and perform his will; he will destroy mighty men and the holy people. And through his shrewdness he will cause deceit to succeed by his influence; and he will magnify himself in his heart, and he will destroy many while they are at ease. He will even oppose the Prince of princes [that is Jesus Christ], but will be broken without human agency (the Book of Daniel 8:23-25).

Persia is modern Iran, and **Byzantium** is modern Turkey. **Versus Serpens** is Latin for a serpent coiled upon itself. It is mentioned in Isaiah 27:1, "Even Leviathan the twisted serpent....the dragon who is in the sea." It denotes Satan who will invade Turkey and Egypt.

This quatrain implies an Islamic takeover in Turkey and Egypt, and a big war between Turkey and Iran.

VESTA'S EXTINGUISHED FIRE TO APPEAR

10:6 "Sardon Nemans si haut déborderont/Qu'on cuidera Deucalion renaître/Dans le colosse la plus part fuiron/Vesta sépulcre feu éteint apparaître.

Sardon Nemans, so high they will overflow
That they will think Deucalion has been reborn.
The majority inside the clossus will flee
[When] the sepulchred Vesta's extinguished fire appears.

Sardon Nemans (or Sardou Nemans in some versions) refers to a modern ruler in Mesopotamia or Iraq. "Sardon" is derived from Sargon, the name of two great rulers in ancient Mesopotamia. Sargon of Akkad built an empire which covered all of Mesopotamia and Syria and reached east to Persia, west to the Mediterranean and north to the Black Sea. Sargon II of Assyria concludes the siege of Samaria, Armenia and Babylonia.

In Greek mythology, **Deucalion** was the sole survivor along with his wife, from a flood. However, the flood and the over-running of borders in this quatrain are a figurative description of an Iraqi power and expansion.

Surprisingly, **Sardon Nemans** is also an anagram for the French spelling of Saddam Hussein: Sadam Housen, if taken into consideration that the letter "H" is a mute one in French, and "Sardon" is given as "Sardou" in other versions.

Moreover, the name "Nemans" is almost similar to the spelling of Haman, the villain who persecuted the Jews in the book of Esther.

Colossus in line three refers to a giant structure, made for sports or as an administrative center, like the Pentagon for example. Nostradamus, by colossus, is making an allusion to Rome, capital of Italy. Ancient Rome was a major sport and administrative center in the Roman Empire.

Line four refers to the release and detonation of nuclear energy. **Vesta** was the protectress goddess of Rome. Her round temple was Rome's hearth. Her fire had been kept burning for more than six hundred years in Rome, until it was put out and the ritual erased by the Christians.

The Fire of Goddess Vesta

THE PUNIC HEART TO INVADE MALTA

1:9 "De l'Orient viendra le coeur Punique/Fâcher Hardrie et les hoires Romulides/Accompagné de la classe Libyque/Trembler Melites et proches îles vides."

The Punic heart will come from the Orient
To trouble Hadria and the heirs of Romulus.
Accompanied by the Libyan fleet,
Malta, trembling, and the nearby islands are deserted.

The **Punic heart** refers to the Arab Anti-Christ from Egypt. The Punic wars were the wars between the Roman empire and the African Carthage under the leadership of Hannibal.

Hadria and Adria (Latin Hadrianus, Adrianus) are the names of two Italian cities. In this quatrain, **Hadria** indicates mainland Italy.

The **heirs of Romulus** are the Italians. Romulus is the mythical founder of Rome, along with his brother Remus. Romulus, after killing Remus, became the first king of Rome. He was later worshipped by the Romans as god, and temples were built in his honor.

The **Libyan fleet** is the fleet of the Anti-Christ coming from the direction of north Africa.

Malta is a country made up of a group of islands in the Mediterranean Sea, south of Sicily. Malta is the main island of this group.

Apparently, the Anti-Christ will devastate Malta on his way to conquer Sicily and Italy.

THE EMERGENCE OF THE WARMONGER

2:5 "Qu'en dans poisson, fer et letre enfermée/Hors sortira qui puis fera la guerre/Aura par mer sa classe bien ramée/Apparaissant près de Latin terre."

When in fish iron and letter are enclosed,
Then the one who will make war shall emerge.
He will have his fleet well staked by sea,
Appearing near Italian land.

The first line refers to the Catholic Church (**fish**) in Italy, or else it is just an allusion to the invention of submarines. Also a conjunction of Mars/Mercury in Pisces is implied.

THE ANGER OF THE IMPOTENT PRINCE

4:4 "L'impotent prince fâché, plaints et querelles/De rapts et pilles par coqs et par Libyque/Grand est par terre, par mer infinies voiles/ Seule Italie sera chassant Celtiques.

The impotent prince is angry. There are complaints and quarrels, Of rapes and pillages committed by the cocks and by Libyans. The land army is great, by sea the sails are numberless. Only from Italy the French will be driven away.

The **impotent prince** is the Arab Anti-Christ. The prophet Daniel also related that he would be impotent. He wrote, "and he will show no regard for....the desire of women" (Daniel 11:37).

The **Libyans** are the Arabs of north Africa. The Egyptians are the **cocks.**

THE WRECKAGE OF A FLEET BY ADRIATIC SEA

2:86 "Naufrage à classe près d'onde Hadriatique/La terre émue sus l'air en terre mis/Egypte tremble augment Mahometique/L'Héraut soi rendre à crier est commis."

A fleet is wrecked near the Adriatic Sea. The land is to tremble when the smoldering in the air is settled on earth. Egypt is to be shaken. Moslem influence will be in increase. The chief, giving himself up, is turned to weeping.

Heraut is the exact word used by Nostradamus for **chief** in line four. He used to be a Roman public official entrusted with the task of proclaiming war. His person was sacrosanct.

MACEDON INVADED BY IRAN

2:96 "Flambeau ardent au ciel soir sera vu/Pres de la fin et pricipe du Rosne/Famine, glaive: tard le secours pourvu/La Perse tourne envahir Macedoine."

A burning flame will be seen in the evening sky,
Near the end and the beginning of the Rhone.
Famine, steel. The help too late provided.
Persia turns to invade Macedon.

A **burning flame** in the sky could indicate a hot missile traversing the sky. The river **Rhone** rises in the Alps, Switzerland, flows into Lake Geneva, issues from the southwest end of the lake, crosses the French border, continues south through Lyon, Avignon, and Tarascon to Arles; empties into the Gulf of Lion, into the Mediterranean Sea, through several branches.

Steel in line three indicates war.

Macedon is an ancient country and kingdom in the Macedonia region, originally located north of Thessaly and northwest of the Aegean Sea. The Macedonian Empire, comprising Macedonia and the countries conquered by Alexander the Great, reached from Macedon beyond the eastern boundaries of former Persian Empire into upper India. As a result of the Second Balkan War 1913, Macedonia was partitioned between Yugoslavia and Greece.

Also, in the first line, the appearance of a comet is implied.

TURKEY AND GREECE ARE INVADED BY IRAN

3:64 "Le chef de Perse remplira grande Olchades/Classe trirème contre gens Mahometique/De Parthe et Mede: et piller les Cyclades/ Repos long temps au grand port Ionique.

The chief of Persia will fold the merchant ships,
He will assemble warships countering a Muhammadan people.
He will come from Parthia and Media to pillage the Cyclades,
And have a long rest at the great Ionic port.

Persia of course is modern Iran. The **Muhammadan people** in line two are the Turks. The Turks are Sunnite Moslems, while the Iranians are Shiite, an Islamic sect opposed to the orthodox Sunnite. Moreover, the Turks and the Iranians are historical enemies to each other.

Parthia and Media are presently parts of modern Iran. The **Cyclades** are a group of about 220 mountainous islands in the Aegean Sea. Presently, they belong to Greece. The **great Ionic port** is modern Istanbul, known historically by the name of Constantinople.

WAR BESIDE RIVER ARAKS NEXT TO ARMENIA AND IRAN

3:31 "Aux champs de Mede, d'Arabe et d'Armenie/Deux grandes copies trois fois s'assembleron/Près du rivage d'Araxes la mesenie/ Du grand Soliman en terre tomberont."

**On the fields of Media, of Arabia, and of Armenia,
Two great armies will assemble three times.
Near the river Araks, the host
Of the great Suleyman will be cut off.**

The country of **Media** was originally the plateau region corresponding to the northwestern part of modern Iran, which was occupied by Medes, an Iranian people. **Armenia** was an ancient country in Western Asia. It centered in the mountainous region (highest point Mt. Ararat) southeast of the Black Sea and southwest of the Caspian Sea, including the sources of the Euphrates and Araks rivers and the lakes Van and Sevan.

Turkish Armenia is the northeastern part of modern Turkey, comprising the whole or parts of nine provinces; about 57,000 sq. miles; the chief towns are Kars, Erzurum, Erzincan.

River Araks (or ancient Araxes) rises in the mountains of Turkish Armenia south of Erzurum, and flows into the Caspian Sea. About half of its course forms the boundary between the republic of Armenia and Azerbaijan on the north and Turkey and northwestern Iran on the south. It is 568 miles long.

The **host of the great Suleyman** is the Turkish army that is going to get involved in the battle near the river Araks. Historically, Suleyman II the Magnificent, was a Turkish Sultan, a contemporary of Nostradamus, who developed the power of the Ottoman Turks to its greatest extent. Coincidentally, the current President of Turkey, whose term of office will expire in 2000, has the name Suleyman Demirel.

On 1988, fighting between Azerbaijan and the Armenian Karabakh Mountain Area erupted and has been going on ever since. Azerbaijan and her ally Turkey have imposed a blockade on the republics of Armenia and Nagorno-Karabakh, putting a halt to much-needed shipments of food, fuel and supplies and leaving the Armenian economy in ruins.

Russia is supplying both sides with military hardware and Azerbaijan is being given weapons by Turkey, England, China and Israel. Also, the Azerbaijani government is paying professional soldiers from Turkey, Afghanistan and the Ukraine to fight for them.

There are fears that "the forgotten war" in the Caucasus will escalate and draw its neighboring countries into the conflict.

In the 19th century, Russia made several unsuccessful runs towards the greener pastures to its south and toward the strategic city of Constantinople (or Istanbul), then the capital of the Ottoman empire. Russia's overtures were checked and frustrated by England, the biggest imperialist power in the nineteen century.

In March '94, in an interview from Moscow with Public Broadcasting's "...Talking with David Frost" show, Zhirinovasky explained his theory of "the dash to the south." He said that the West should stay clear of the former Soviet Union, Turkey, Iran, and Afghanistan. He put the emphasis on those last three countries, saying that they should be reserved for Russia's so-called dash (or push, or march) to the south, in their search for warmer climates. In fact, Zhirinovsky is merely reflecting the real views of the Russian military and intelligence agencies. The Russians, sooner or later, will implement the futuristic policies expounded by Zhirinovosky, with or without Zhirinovsky being in the reign of power.

In his book "The Last Dash to the South" Zhirinovsky writes that "nothing will happen to the world even if the entire Turkish nation perishes....Let the Turks remember how they came to Asia Minor [modern Turkey], barbarously seized Constantinople [now Istanbul] and plundered it, and butchered and subjugated all the peoples."

A look at the map of the Middle East (where the fuse of World War III is going to be ignited) shows that Russia needs the alliance of the Arabs in order to mount a twin pincers attack or to just put pressure on the countries which are situated between them. Zhirinovsky once mentioned giving his Arab friends nuclear weapons. There is no doubt that, if this alliance is materialized, it will reshape the Middle East and western Asia and will alter both political and pshychological maps of the region.

At a time when Russia is in crisis at just about every front: political, economic, social and religious, and the Russians feel weak and incapable of attending to their needs, they will normally start looking for a strong leader who could take them out of their morass and lead them to become a world power once more. There was a time when the Russians thought that they had found their man in Boris Yeltsin, but he turned out to be a disappointment. Naturally, now they will look for another strong man and put him in charge. There is a great possibility that the dictatorial Zhirinovsky (or his political equivalent), with full backing of the Russian military, will fill that vacuum and make of Russia a new world power.

TREBIZOND IN TURKEY IS OCCUPIED

5:27 "Par feu et armes non loin de la marnegro/Viendra de Perse occuper Trebisonde/Trembler Pharos, Methelin, Sol alegro/De sang Arabe d'Adrie couvert onde."

By firepower of armies, not far from the Black Sea,
He will come from Persia to occupy Trebizond.
Pharos, Mytilene, and the vivid Sun will tremble.
The waves of the Adriatic Sea will be covered with Arab blood.

This quatrain refers to the Anti-Christ who will invade eastern Turkey from Iran (**Persia**). Then a tremor will go through Egypt (**Pharos**), through Greece (**Mytiline**), and through the brilliant sun. The war will spread to Europe where the Adriatic Sea will be littered with the dead bodies of Arab soldiers.

Trebizond is the ancient name of Trabzon, a province and a city in northeastern Turkey by the Black Sea.

The Greek Empire of Trebizond (1204-1478) included, at its greatest, Georgia, Crimea, and the entire southern shore of the Black Sea east of the Sakarya river.

Pharos is a peninsula near Alexandria, Egypt, whose lighthouse once was one of the seven wonders of the world. It was demolished by an earthquake, 1302. **Mytilene** or Mitilini is a Greek port on the island of Lesbos. The **vivid sun** smitten by a tremor signifies a clouded and dark future.

THE WORLD IS PUT INTO TROUBLE BY THREE ALLIES

8:17 "Les bien aises subit seront demis/Par les trois freres le monde mis en trouble/Cite marine saisiront ennemis/Faim, feu, sang, pest, et de tous maux le double."

The well-off suddenly will be brought low.
The world is put into trouble by three brothers.
The enemy will seize the maritime city.
Famine, fire, blood, plague, and double of all evils.

Nostradamus is announcing World War III in this quatrain. First of all, he says, those in high places of leadership will be toppled from power, and those who would be enjoying the good life will suddenly find their fortune turn for the worse.

Three allies (**brothers**) will start the World War; most likely the Arab Anti-Christ along with the leaders of Iran and Russia.

The enemies of France will take over Marseille (**the maritime city**). And the use of biological and chemical warfare along with the conventional warfare shall cause hunger, fire, blood, plague and other evils to come upon mankind in double measure.

A BIG WAR IN EUROPE IN THE SUMMER OF TWO ECLIPSES

8:15 "Vers Aquilon grands efforts par homasse/Presque l'Europe et l'Universe vexer/Les deux eclipses mettra en telle chasse/Et aux Pannons vie et mort renforcer."

Toward Aquilon the great efforts by massed troops
Almost to vex Europe and the Universe.
The two eclipses will follow [each other] so close,
And reinforce life and death in Pannonia.

In the first French line, **hommes masse** (=a great body of men) is condensed to **homasse** by Nostradamus for rhyming purpose.

Aquilon is the North (or the north wind); in this quatrain it indicates Russia whose mobilized armies and belligerent attitude are to alarm Europe and the rest of the world.

Already, the new Russian military doctrine (published on November 1993) leaves no doubt that military power will remain an important instrument of Russian policy for years to come. It also raises the potential of Russia becoming once more a menace to the West, since Russia's new military doctrine calls for abandonment of its no-first-use pledge of nuclear weapons. Furthermore, in the new policy, Russia reserves the right to launch nuclear strikes in response not only to a conventional attack on Russia Federation territory, on CIS allies and Russian forces abroad, but also to a conventional attack carried out by a non-nuclear country, if that country has an alliance agreement with a nuclear country. Also, actions taken to destroy or disrupt Russian strategic nuclear forces, the early warning system, nuclear power and chemical installations, are all considered enemy "attack," with Russia reserving the right to strike back with nuclear weapons in response. Needless to say, Russia already has shelved its plans to half their military personnel by 1995.

A new alarming factor is the revelations made about Russia's super secret weaponry. In an interview broadcast on February 1994 by the TV show: 60 MINUTES, Zhirinovsky made allusions to secret weapons, more destructive than nuclear weapons, now in the possession of Russia. He answered the interviewer in his broken English thusly: "Elipton, sonar, very effective weapons. Elipton is light, for example, LASER, large light, it destroys all. Laser light destroys all: Building, people, way, transportation, communication, all. Sonar weapon is noise, very big noise, for it is impossible for people to support, to survive, it is very big noise." In answer to a question if he had seen pictures of those weapons, he answered in affirmative and said that he had even been shown the hardware by the Russian military and shown how they can be used.

It is amazing how Mother Mary revealed (in a locution through Veronica Lueken, given on July 25, 1985) the existence of the laser weapons in Russia which "emit long streams of light, disintegrating and melting everything." Mother Mary stated: "Russia, My children, has this implement of destruction. While the United States and Canada and most of the world go about crying for peace, tranquility, love, they are not aware of the fact that Russia has every mind to take them over, be it good or bad. And if they have to annihilate the whole land of its people, they want that land, and they will use any means to get it."

Other sources have also indicated that the purpose of the Russian military is to fight a war against the United States that will be over so fast (in a few days) that the NATO powers will find it meaningless to go to war after the USA is destroyed. In fact, a coordinated Russian surprise first attack on America could render the USA incapable of an effective response.

The resurgent nationalism and imperialism in Russia has its roots in the Russian Pan-Slavic ideology which was originally conceived in the will of Peter the Great. That will outlines the plan for the subjugation of Europe (and, by extension, now the USA) by Russian Slavs. In the 19th century, that Russian ideology sent shivers through England—the biggest imperialist power then—which did its utmost to keep czarist Russia in check.

The **two eclipses** in line three are those of the year 1999. A July 28 lunar eclipse and an August 11 total solar eclipse; the first total solar eclipse for central Europe since 1961, but best viewing should be in Iran and Iraq; southeastern Europe and Turkey should also offer a good view.

Pannonia was the name of the Roman province that included territory now mostly in Hungary and former Yugoslavia.

JULY or SEPTEMBER 1999

10:72 "L'an mil neuf cent nonante neuf sept mois/Du ciel viendra un grand Roi d'effrayeur/Ressusciter le grand Roi d'Angolmois/Avant apres Mars regner par bonheur."

In the seventh month of the year 1999,
A great King of terror will come from the sky.
The great King of Angolmois is resuscitated [in 1999].
Before and after [1999], Mars [=war] to reign freely.

The **seventh month** may well be counted from Nostradamus' contemporary New Year: The spring equinox of 20/21 March.

Nostradamus had Hebrew background. The Jews believe that it was "a king of terror coming from the sky" that brought the series of plagues upon the Egyptians, some 3600 years ago, when the Pharaoh refused his Hebrew slaves to go free with Moses to the promised land.

In Dec. 1993, astronomers spotted a planet heading our way. They called it Planet X. According to Z. Sitchin, the ancient Sumerians wrote about a planet of our solar system having an eccentric orbit of 3600 years—visiting earth at 3600 year interval. The Sumerians indicated that this planet is inhabited by gods (space people) who created modern humanity.

Will Earth have an encounter with Planet X and the gods in 1999?

C.1, Q.91 states: "The gods [=the space people] will appear to the humans./To warn that the humans will start the great conflict [=WW 3]./Before the heaven finishes [its warning] sword and lance will engage [=the war will start]./Oh that those of the left hand [=the black magicians who are responsible for the war] be greatly afflicted!"

"Les Dieux feront aux humains apparence./Ce qu'ils seront auteurs de grand conflict./Avant ciel vu serein: épée et lance./Que vers main gauche sera plus grand afflict."

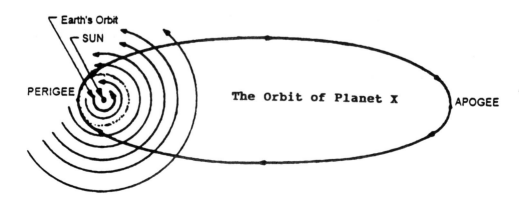

Earth's Orbit
SUN
PERIGEE
The Orbit of Planet X
APOGEE

Angolmois in line three has been interpreted as an anagram for "Mongolois," which means Mongols in old French.

The historical King of the Mongols is Attila (c406–453), who claimed dominion from the Alps and the Baltic to the Caspian Sea. From 441–50 he ravaged the Eastern Roman Empire as far as Constantinople and invaded Gaul in 451 reaching the region of Angouleme, this expedition earning him the title of "Scourge of God." The following year he invaded Italy, but retired without attacking Rome.

The third line has an alternate interpretation. By **the great king of Angolmois** Nostradamus is also making a reference to the warrior French king Francis I (1494–1547), king of France from 1515, who was also count of Angouleme (Angoulmois was a province of France in the Middle Ages). Francis I spend 23 years of his reign fighting the Holy Roman Empire. He conducted costly wars against the Hapsburgs, including abortive Italian campaigns.

Apparently, on July 1999, the "great king of terror who will come from the sky" will resuscitate the memory of King Francis I by making war against the revived Holy Roman Empire, namely the European Union.

THE KING OF THE ORIENT TO SUBJUGATE THE WEST

Presage No. 40 "De maison sept par mort mortelle suite/Grêle, tempatê, pestilent; mal, fureurs/Roi d'Orient d'Occident tous en fuite/Subjuguera ses jadis conquereurs."

**Of the seventh house, followed by mortal death, will issue
Hail, tempest, pestilence, evil furies.
All the West is put to flight by the King of the Orient,
Who will subjugate [the Orient's] former conquerors.**

In Astrology, the ups and downs of life are divided into twelve divisions called the Twelve Houses. The seventh is the house of marriage and partnership. The eighth is the house of death and regeneration. This presage implies that from the breakdown of friendship and alliance between the East and the West, will follow death, hail, tempest and evil furies.

• • •

In an interview given to *TIME* (May 8, 1995, page 76), Boris Yeltsin said: "Theoretically, such a danger (of Russia sliding back into authoritarianism) exists. We are only beginning to build our democratic state and new economy. Given our history, these are extremely hard tasks, and we are forced to pursue both goals at the same time. We do not have any other options. A strong civic society, a middle class and a culture of law are basic conditions for a stable democracy in any country. But these preconditions are only taking shape in Russia. For these reasons, the danger of an authoritarian regime will exist here for some time yet. Two scenarios for sliding into authoritarianism are possible. The first one would come about from the degeneration of the present regime. The second would be a takeover by forces who stand for a communist revenge or for aggressive nationalism."

• • •

Recent polls taken in Russia have indicated that the popular nationalist army general Alexandr Lebed is one of the two men, along with Mr. Zyuganov, most likely to become president of Russia in 1996.

Gen. Lebed, 45, is an Afghan war hero and anti-establishment person. His nationalist rhetoric is pungent, but his views are more sensible than the bizarre threats of Mr. Zhirinovsky, the extreme nationalist.

The retired General harbors a deep mistrust of NATO and the West. He wants the restoration of the Russian empire and says that it's time to bring back a little Soviet-style order and discipline to Russia. "We Russians are doomed to live in an authoritarian state until genuine democracy, which should not be confused with anarchy, can be set up," he said recently.

Presently the Russians are angry at the grubby, lawless state of their nation. They are weary of corruption, organized crime and fallen pride. They are looking forward to a strong leadership and a new face—with a touch of the iron-fisted authority of old.

Recently, a Russian newspaper editor said: "Of course the pendulum is going to swing back. But the real question for Russia is how far will it go."

The Communists already made a comeback in Russia. They now control virtually a third of Russia's new Parliament; and Gennadi Zyuganov, the Communist leader, declared that it was time to start planning for the Presidential race of 1996.

• • •

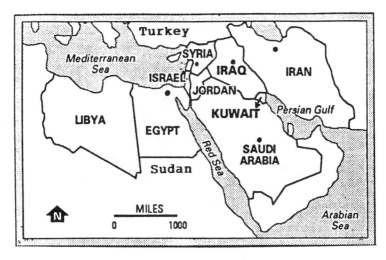

THE HOT SPOT: FORMER YUGOSLAVIA

A Hot Spot: Caucasus - Where the power play for regional control is between Russia, Turkey, Iran and the West.

"And they worshiped the dragon which gave power unto the beast (the Third Anti-Christ); and they worshiped the beast..."

Revelation 13:4, KJV

THE VISIONS OF DANNION BRINKLEY

Mr. Brinkley had two remarkable near-death experiences. In his book, *Saved by the Light—The True Story of a Man Who Died Twice and the Profound Revelations He Received* (Villard Books/Random House Inc., 1994), he mentions prophetic visions given to him while in Heaven in his spiritual body about events that would shake the world before the year 2000.

One vision indicated two horrendous earthquakes occurring in the USA sometimes before the end of the century, and as a result of those catastrophes the role of America as a world power coming to an end.

Another vision indicates that by the turn of the century, the world would be in a horrible turmoil, giving way to a feudalistic New World Order full of strife.

In brief vision he saw Egypt being taken over by religious fanatics by the year 1997.

He also saw, in a vision, a new kind of computer chip being manufactured in the Middle East and Asia from biological components, those new computer chips are used in every form of technology. They are even used for marking and cataloging human beings; the chips being inserted under the skin. This system of control is implemented by a new emerging dictator from the Middle East.

His final visions were about a horrible World War III. He writes: "Scenes from WW III came to life before me. I was in a hundred places at once, from deserts to forests, and saw a world filled with fighting and chaos. Somehow it was clear that this final war, an Armaggedon if you will, was caused by fear. In one of the most puzzling visions of all, I saw an army of women in black robes and veils [= Moslems] marching through a European city."

He was told the world by the year 2004 will not be the same one we now know if we follow the same dogma and live the same pattern of life-style.

ISLAMIC FUNDAMENTALISM

In recent years Islamic fundamentalism has been sweeping like a scourge over a great part of the third world, to the point where Islamic militancy has become the principle adversary of the West in the post-cold-war years. Even NATO, early in 1995, had to issue a statement saying that the organization must now turn its attention to fighting Islamic fundamentalism.

Islamic militants believe that the Islamic renaissance has to be born out of blood, and that only by striking at the West will Islam ever be able to dictate events in the world and avenge the humiliations Moslems are said to have suffered at the hands of the West.

In the Middle East and north Africa the militants are working for the overthrow of secular Arab regimes in order to establish an Islamic pan-Arab empire and an international Moslem brotherhood.

If Arabs, Persians and others unite they could easily destroy Israel and march on right to western Europe. Communist China is preparing to become a superpower; she is using foreign technology in both the private and military sectors for its new emergence into the world within a decade. The Chinese are going to be allies with the Arabs.

The Moslem militants do not love God. They consider Islam the elevator to take power.

The coming Arab Anti-Christ will shake up the Islamic religion (along with the Christian religion). Thursday is going to be an important day to him and his followers.

"One individual, in darkness of spirit and insanity of sin, shall set mankind into a major war that shall bring about the destruction and annihilation of nations."

"You will all recognize the signs of him who seeks to destroy, he will have on his coat of Arms the Half Moon Sickle."

Prophecies from OUR LADY OF THE ROSES SHRINE, in Bayside, New York, USA.

44 •

THE FIRST

THE SECOND

THE THIRD

Chapter 3

THE COMING THIRD ANTI-CHRIST

• • • • • • • • • • • • • • • • •

In his prophecies, Nostradamus mentioned three main Anti-Christs who would ravage his beloved France. The first Anti-Christ was Napoleon Bonaparte. After ruling France with an iron fist, Napoleon set out to conquer and rule the world. He failed. Nostradamus' predictions about him were 100 percent accurate.

The second Anti-Christ was Hitler who had a short reign full of death and madness. He plunged the earth into World War II. His goal was to conquer and rule the world. He also failed. Again Nostradamus' predictions about him were remarkably accurate.

The coming third Anti-Christ - according to Nostradamus - will be an Arab despot from the Middle East. He will plunge the planet earth into World War III. His goal will be to rule the world. He will surely and miserably fail.

First, he will appear as a political leader in Egypt in order to fulfill - in his own eyes - that which was spoken by God through the prophet: "Out of Egypt did I call My Son." He will consider himself to be the true Messiah. His "ministry" will start when he is about thirty years old, just like Jesus who began His Ministry when about thirty years of age, (Luke 3:23).

In the first line of quatrain No. 79 (of century No. 8), Nostradamus mentions the Anti-Christ's father being killed during an Arab-Israeli war (most likely in the six day war of 1967) leaving behind his two-year-old male child in custody of a religious order ("be raised in a nunnery") or a religious relative. The second line of quatrain No. 54 (of century No. 10) reads: "When two years old he is taken on by the sad news" of the death of his father. Hence, by adding the number thirty (his age when he will make himself known to the world) to the year 1965 (his most likely date of birth), then an approximate date of his rise to power can be figured; sometime between 1995 and 1997.

In his prophecies, Nostradamus indicated the Third Anti-Christ by various appellations and adjectives, such as: The oriental king, the Arab prince, the great one, the king, beast , the dark man, the red one, the azure, the barbarian chief, the monster of Tarascon, the third, he, the seline, the punic heart, "Raypoz," and other names.

A trance interpretation by Paul Shockley from a source which identifies itself as "Cosmic Awareness" said in a reading given in 1993 that the Third Anti-Christ "may begin to gradually be brought into focus during this year and over a period of three years, whereby by the end of approximately the third year, around 1995 or 1996, that his entity would rise to a position well-viewed internationally, and while the entity's words and appearance can be very charismatic and promising in terms of being likened unto a peacemaker, this entity's later actions would be very detrimental to the masses of the earth. This Awareness indicates it appears that most countries will accept this entity as a kind of new Messiah or spiritual leader and also political leader, but that Russia, the United States and Canada generally will not buy into the promotion of this entity. There will be some, of course, in these countries who do, and some in other countries who don't accept this entity as a kind of Messiah, but this entity will create extreme problems for most of the world before he is brought down. He will appear to be a savior, or one who can bring peace and economic well-being to the world as he rises in power.

"The entity has studied, the entity was born in Egypt, has studied business, has studied politics, has studied religion, and is being carefully tutored. The entity is being given background in various religion, being taught how they all have similar connections or parallels and this entity will focus on these parallels in such a way that each religions will feel he represents them, or at least, that is the intention of his training, to give that feeling, so that no matter where he is, or what religion he speaks to, others from other religions will think that he is teaching their religion to the heathens, even though those who he speaks to may think that he is teaching their own religion in a more global and all-inclusive way. He will appear to speak little and say much with the words issued. It will be more his followers who speak in his behalf and the entity's gradual ascension on the stage of life in the media will begin to be felt more in 1994, '95 and '96.

"This Awareness asks you to be very discerning and attentive to any who claim to be a Messiah. The entity will, in the end be much more of a thread to humanity than were the two previous antichrists: Napoleon and Hitler. This Awareness indicates the term 'antichrist' for these entities is not perhaps a correct label though it has been historically presented to these entities by theologians who were waiting and expecting the antichrist and saw these entities as representing the antichrists. This Awareness indicates that the entity Napoleon created, in a single action, a separation of church and state. When he was to be crowned king of France by the church, he reached out and took the crown from the hands of the Cardinal who was preparing to crown him, and put it on his own head. Thus doing, he symbolically took power from the church and gave it to the state, to himself, as head of the state or King of France. When he gave himself power, rather than allowing the church to give the power to him, it was the beginning of separation of church and state in this regard. This Awareness indicates that for this, there were many who saw him as a challenge to the church, a challenge to religion and called him an antichrist. His further deeds and actions, taking war to many lands, contributed also to those arguments that he was an antichrist. Of course, those who know of Adolf Hitler, realize he was a manic/depressive who had psychotic tendencies and was basically mentally sick and not actually a greatly intelligent person. He was not really an antichrist so much as a mentally insane person trying to run the country with megalomaniacal dreams of world conquest.

"This Awareness indicates the new antichrist will be much more sophisticated than either of these and his influence will be smoother and more well-controlled. He will not necessarily be the power behind the throne; there will be other powers behind him that are truly pulling the strings. He will be a world puppet playing the role of an extremely sophisticated world leader. This Awareness indicates it will also be at a time when the number system and marketing system on individuals has been introduced. A world currency will also be introduced and money in the world currency backed by gold will be promoted at that time, so that this entity will accompany the development of the world economic system and New World Order and control of nations. This Awareness indicates however, as previously suggested, the United States, Russia and Canada appear to be unwilling to accept this and eventually will bring down his power. (Revelations of Awareness, issue No. 429, March 1994, page 14,—P.O. Box 115, Olympia, WA 98507, USA).

The book "Conversations with Nostradamus" by Dolores Cannon also attests that the coming Arab Anti-Christ "will appear on the world scene at a time when nations will be going through economical hardships...he will assign to each person a number and print it indelibly by laser on the hand or the forehead The scanning of the number would be necessary in order to shop or enter an official building. Those who refuse to be part of his diabolical system will be outcast (Revelation 13:16, 17)....a great orator, he will be able to attract the populace to himself; and through smooth speech, seductive words and flatteries, he will win over the rulers of the world."

CHAPTER 17 OF THE BOOK OF REVELATION

(FOR THE TESTIMONY OF JESUS IS THE SPIRIT OF PROPHECY. Rev. 19:10)

And one of the seven angels who had the seven bowls came with me, saying, "Come here, I shall show you the judgment of the great harlot (= Ancient Rome) who sits on many waters (= people and nations), with whom the kings of the earth committed acts of immorality, and those who dwell on the earth were made drunk with the wine of her immorality.

And he carried me away in the Spirit into a wilderness; and I saw - a woman sitting on a scarlet beast (= the empire of the Third Anti-Christ), full of blasphemous names, having seven heads and ten horns. And the woman (= the empire) was clothed in purple and scarlet, and adorned with gold and precious stones and pearls, having in her hand a gold cup full of abominations and of the unclean things of her immortality, and upon her forehead a name was written, a mystery, "BABYLON THE GREAT, THE MOTHER OF HARLOTS AND OF THE ABOMINA-TIONS OF THE EARTH." And I saw the woman (= the empire) drunk with the blood of the saints, and with the blood of the witnesses of Jesus. And when I saw her, I wondered greatly.

And the angel said to me, "Why do you wonder? I shall tell you the mystery of the woman and the beast that carries her, which has seven heads and the ten horns. The beast (= the Anti-Christ) that you saw was and is not, and is about to come up out of the abyss and to go to destruction. And those who dwell on the earth wonder, whose name has not been written in the bcok of life from the foundation of the world, when they see the beast, that he was and is not and will come. Here is the mind which has widsom. The seven heads are seven mountains (= Kingdoms, empires) on which the woman sits, and they are seven kings; five (= those of ancient Egypt, Assyria, Babylon, Medo-Persia and ancient Greek) have fallen, one (= the Roman empire) is, and the other (= the Nazi empire of Hitler) has not yet come; and when he comes he must remain a little while. And the beast which was and is not, is himself also an eighth (= the coming empire of the Third Anti-Christ) and is one of the seven, and he goes to destruction.

"And the ten horns which you saw are ten kings (= ten rulers in the Middle east and north Africa), who have not yet received a kingdom, but they receive authority as kings with the beast for one hour. These have one purpose and they give their power and authority to the beast (= the Third Anti-Christ). These will wage against the Lamb (= Jesus Christ and the Christians), and the Lamb will overcome them, because He is Lord of Lords and King of Kings, and those who are with Him are the called and the chosen and the faithful."

And he said to me, "The waters which you saw where the Harlot (= ancient Rome, the capital of the Roman empire) sits (at the time when the Book of Revelation was written), are people and multitudes and nations and tongues. And the ten horns (= ten rulers from the Middle East and Africa) which you saw, and the beast (= their leader, the Third Anti-Christ), these will hate the harlot (modern Rome and the Vatican) and will make her desolate and naked, and will eat her flesh and burn her up with fire. For God has put it in their hearts to execute His purpose by giving their kingdom to the beast, until the words of God should be fulfilled.

"And the woman who you saw is the great city (= the empire of the Anti-Christ/the Great Babylon), which reigns over the kings of the earth."

HIS HUMBLE BIRTH ON A DARK DAY

10:9 "De Castillon figuieres jour de brume/De Femme infame naîtra souverain prince/Surnome de chausses perhume lui posthume/Onc Roi ne fut si pire en sa province."

From a figurine castle on a dark day,
The sovereign prince will be born of a common woman.
A surname of breeches is given to him after his [father's] death.
Never was there a king so very bad in his province.

The birth of the Anti-Christ - **the sovereign prince** - will not be in a castle. His birth will be in a "figurine/phony castle," in other words, he will be born in humble surroundings. His mother will not be a queen, but a common infamous woman.

After the death of his father, a "royal" surname is bestowed upon his. "Chausses" means breeches or stockings in French, apparently his new name has something to do with breeches. In any way, his new surname means that he is adopted by prominent people.

Line four refers to his performance when in power as ruler of the new Arab empire.

HE IS BORN IN JERUSALEM

5:84 "Naitra du gouffre et cité immesurée/Né de parents obscurs et ténébreaux/Qui la puissance du grand Roi révérée/Voudra détruire par Roüen et Eureux."

He will be born of the abyss and in the unmeasured city,
From obscure and dark parents;
He who the dominion of the great reverend King,
Will want to destroy up to Rouen and Evreux.

The Arab Anti-Christ - whose coming is from the bottomless pit - is to be born in the holy city of Jerusalem (**the unmeasured city**) from obscure and secretive parents. The unmeasured city is Jerusalem according to a verse in the Bible. Revelation 11:2 reads: "And leave out the court which is outside the temple, and do not measure it...." Before the 1967 Arab-Israeli War the old part of Jerusalem was under Jordanian administration.

The **great reverend King** in line three is the Catholic Pope whose dominion and power in Europe the Arab Anti-Christ will try to destroy all the way to north France. (**Rouen** is a dynamic cultural, commercial and industrial center in Normandy, France. **Evreux** is a smaller city near Rouen.)

HE IS TO LOSE HIS FATHER IN WAR

8:79 "Qui par fer père perdra né de Nonnaire/De Gorgon sur là fera sang perfetant/En terre étrange fera si tout de taire/Qui brûlera lui-même et son enfant."

One who will lose his father by iron and be raised in nunnery,
Upon him, from Gorgon, the blood will fall.
In foreign land he will do the unspeakable,
Even burning himself and his child.

The Arab Anti-Christ - his soldier father being a casualty of war (**iron**) - will be raised under religious guidance and custody (**nunnery**). The death of his father is most likely in the 1967 Arab-Israeli War in which Israel, after defeating the Jordanian army took over the Old City.

Gorgons are female mythical monsters in Greek mythology. They symbolize evil and negative energies. The second line implies that the evil one will saddle the Anti-Christ with the task of administering the negative Karma or the bad debt of humanity on planet earth. His deeds are going to be so indescribable; he will not care whether he or his empire (**his child**) gets hurt and burned up in the process of performing his insane acts.

HE IS BORN OF A SECRET MISTRESS

10:54 "Née en ce monde par concubine furtive/À deux haut mise par les triste nouvelle/Entre ennemis sera prise captive/Et amenée à Malings et Bruxelles."

He is born in this world of a secret mistress.
When two years old he is taken on by the sad news.
He will be taken prisoner by his enemies,
And brought to Malines and Brussels.

The **sad news** is the death of the father of the Anti-Christ when he is a mere child of two years old.

Later on, when he is an adult, he will be taken prisoner by his enemies and brought to Malines and Brussels.

Malines or modern Mechelen (or Mechlin) is a city in north Belgium. It enjoyed great prosperity in 15th and early 16th centuries. **Brussels** is the capital of Belgium where presently the European Union headquarters building is located.

HIS CAPTIVITY AND SUBSEQUENT RELEASE

4:34 "Le grand mené captive d'étrange terre/D'or enchainé au roi CHYREN offert/Qui dans Ausonne, Millan perdra la guerre/Et tout son ost mis à feu et à fer."

The great one is made captive of a foreign land.
In golden chains he is offered to the king of CHYREN.
He who in Ausonia and Milan will lose the war
And all his army be destroyed by fire and iron.

The Arab Anti-Christ (**the great one**) after losing the war in Italy, and the total annihilation of his army, is taken prisoner. He is ransomed by the ruler of CHYRIN. **Chyrin** is an anagram for Cyrene, the original capital of Cyrenaica; easternmost part of Libya in north Africa. The city was founded by Greeks c.630 B.C.

Milan is a commercial and industrial commune, capital of Lombardy and of the Milano province, in northern Italy. **Ausonia** is the area about Naples in Italy. Mount Ausoni is located between Naples and Rome.

It seems that Anti-Christ's first blunder will be his first campaign against Italy. His army will go up in smoke, he will be wounded, taken captive then ransomed and released. In chapter 13 of the book of Revelation there is an accurate description of his amazing recovery. Verse 3 reads: "And I saw one of his heads as if had been slain, and his fatal wound was healed. And the whole earth was amazed and followed after the beast." Verses 12 and 14 also refer to the same theme.

THE COMING BACK

5:69 "Plus ne sera le grand en faux sommeil/L'inquiétude viendra prendre repos/Dresser phalange d'or, azur et vermeil/Subjuguer Afrique la ronger jusques aux os."

No longer will the great one be in false sleep;
His solicitude will give way to easiness.
Raising an army of gold, azure and vermillion,
He will subjugate Africa and eat her up to the bone.

After a period of inactivity (**false sleep**), the Anti-Christ will cast his hesitation and worry away. He will raise a strong, heavy and Islamic (**golden, azure**) army and conquer Africa.

HE WILL EXPAND HIS PROMONTORY

9:60 "Conflict Barbare en la Cornette noire/Sang épandu trembler la Dalmatie/Grand Ismael mettra son promontoire/Ranes trembler secours Lusitanie."

A Barbary conflict in the black corner.
Blood is shed. Dalmatia is to tremble.
The great Ishmael will expand his promontory.
The Lusitanian succor will tremble the frogs.

Barbary is coastal region in northern Africa, extending from Egypt to the Atlantic Ocean. The **black corner** refers to Africa. **Dalmatia** is modern Croatia and Bosnia.

The **great Ishmael** is the Arab Anti-Christ. Ishmael (Ismail in Arabic), the immediate patriarch of the North Arabians, was the eldest son of Abraham by Hagar, the Egyptian handmaid of Sarah. (Genesis 16:15).

According to Islamic tradition the descendants of Ishmael are the North Arabians, including the prophet Muhammad himself.

There is also a religious/political sect in the Middle East known as the Ismailis or the Ismailites. A branch of the Ismailities, by the name the "Seveners," came to power in Egypt and parts of Africa, under the Fatimid rulers (909-1171). They followed a popular ideology of collectivism and pursued a program of political insurrection. They had a secret religion, differing from orthodox Islam radically on several vital points. Their doctrines encouraged submission to the authority of a leader or master and abandonment of outward religious practices, because according to their understanding the presence of a divinely guided or a divine leader makes the religious laws superfluous. The "Seveners" believe that they can overcome and rule the world by superior organization and power.

The Ismailites regard themselves as heirs to the inward and secret truth of all religions. Although the sect is usually considered to be a Shiite branch of Islam, in reality is a manifestation within Islam of ancient Persian religious systems. In this sect, even when outward Islam is observed, it is modified to accommodate the inner and essential doctrines of Ismailism.

Basically, Ismailism is a Gnostic-dualist creed which teaches that out of an unknowable God, because of "an inner conflict" between good and evil within Divinity Itself, a series of emanations called "intellects" emerged which culminated in the creation of the world where light and darkness are mixed. And it is said that at the end of the world, light and darkness, which in themselves are neither evil or good, are resolved into their separate domains, while the chosen ones awaken to the realization of their true nature of light and thereby are saved.

The **frogs** in line four are the Egyptians [see Psalm 105:30]. **Lusitania** is an ancient name for Portugal. In this quatrain it refers to the NATO powers.

HE WILL APPEAR IN ASIA

10:75 "Tant attendu ne reviendra jamais/Dedans l'Europe, en Asie apparaîtra/Un de la ligue issue du grand Hermés/Et sur tout Rois des Orient croîtra."

The so long expected one will never come
From inside Europe. He will appear in Asia.
He will be from the league issued from the great Hermes
And will rise high above all the kings of the Orient.

Hermes was known to be the son of Zeus. He was the Greek god who conducted the souls to the dark kingdom of Hades, the underworld. He was also known as the deity of wealth, god of trade and commerce, of manual skill, oratory and eloquence, of thieves, and of the wind—with whose speed he was able to move. Sometimes, he was called the god of Mercury.

(Hermes Trismegistus—Hermes three times the greatest—was a master of alchemical philosophy from Alexandria, Egypt, and a divinity of the Greek colonists in ancient Egypt.)

THE WORSHIP OF THE ANTI-CHRIST ON THURSDAYS

10:71 "La terre, l'air geleront si grand eau/Lorsqu'on viendra pour jeudy vénérer/Ce qui sera jamais ne fut si beau/Des quatre parts le viendront honorer."

The land and the sea will freeze great amounts of water,
When they will come to worship in Thursdays
The one whose image will always seem so fair;
From four directions they will pay homage to him.

The first line could be a reference to literal widespread cold spells or just be figurative speech.

The **worshippers in Thursdays** are the followers of the Anti-Christ, who will be so stunning that multitudes from everywhere will come to pay homage to him.

Verse 7 & 8 of Chapter 13 from the book of Revelation correlate the above prediction of Nostradamus. They read: "And it was given to him to make war with the saints and to overcome them; and authority over tribes and people and tongues and nations was given to him. And all who dwell on earth will worship him, everyone whose name has not been written from the foundation of the world in the book of life of the Lamb [that is Jesus Christ] who has been slain."

THE INVASION OF EUROPE FROM AFRICA AND ASIA

6:80 "De fez le regne parviendra a ceux d'Europe/Feu leur cite et lame tranchera/Le grand d'Asie terre et mer a grande troupe/Que bleus, pers, croix a mort dechassera."

From Fez the realm will reach the nations of Europe.
They will burn their cities and put the inhabitants to sword.
The great one of Asia will lead by land and sea a great army.
Oh that the cross would drive the blue and perse ones to death!

Fez or Fes is a sacred city of Islam in northern central Morocco. The **blue and perse** (dark grayish blue) **ones** are the Moslems and their allies who will invade Europe, burn the cities and kill its inhabitants. The **great one of Asia** is the Anti-Christ who will rally a great naval and land army in order to invade Europe.

The **cross** in line four refers to Christianity under siege.

ANTI-CHRIST TO REIGN LESS THAN 29½ YEARS

9:73 "Dans Fois entrez Roy cerulee Turban/Et regnera moins évolu Saturne/Roy Turban blanc et Bizance coeur ban/Sol, Mars, Mercure ensemble près la hurne."

The King with the azure turban will enter Foix
And reign less than one revolution of Saturn.

The turbanned king will banish the white and Byzantium from his heart.
Sun, Mars, Mercury are together near the urn.

The **king with the azure turban** is the Moslem Arab Anti-Christ. **Foix** is a small town near Toulouse in France. It looks like an enormous rock bristling with towers. Hence Foix stands for tower in this quatrain. The entering of the king into the tower signifies oppression and havoc in the language of Tarot.

Saturn, the sixth planet from the Sun, takes 29½ years to complete one orbit around the Sun.

The **white and Byzantium** in line four refers to Christians whom the Anti-Christ will hate strongly.

The **urn** refers to the vessel of the Waterbearer of the sign Aquarius. Line four is an allusion to an astrological conjunction of Mars, Mercury and the Sun in Aquarius.

THE WARS OF ANTI-CHRIST TO LAST FOR 27 YEARS

8:77 "L'antechrist trois bien tot annihiles/Vingt et sept ans sang durera sa guerre/Les heretique morts, captifs, exiles/Sang, corps human, eau rougie, greler terre."

Very soon the Anti-Christ will destroy three.
His war will last for twenty seven bloody years.
The dissenters are put to death, taken prisoners and are exiled.
Blood, human corpses, water reddened, earth ravaged by hail.

The anti-Christ, soon after he comes to power in Egypt, will usurp and destroy three countries (most likely the north African nations of Algeria, Tunisia, and Morocco). His wars will last for twenty seven years. His opponents are killed, imprisoned and exiled; human blood is shed abundantly.

In his Epistle to the King, Nostradamus gives more details about the wars of the Third Anti-Christ. An excerpt reads: "Behind the Anti-Christ will be the infernal prince [Satan], again for the last time all the kingdoms of Christianity and also those of the infidels will tremble for the space of twenty-five years. There will be more grievous wars and battles; towns, cities, castles, and all other buildings will be burned, desolated, and destroyed, with great effusion of vestal blood. Married woman and widows are violated, children on milk are dashed and bruised against the walls of towns. So many evils will be committed through Satan, the infernal prince, that almost the universal world shall find itself undone and desolate."

Bible expositors have concluded that this emerging Anti-Christ will first of all conquer three countries of the original ten and then take control of the entire group of ten nations. The other seven leaders will yield control of their countries to this new strong man of the Middle East.

They based their conclusions on verses 23 & 24 of Chapter Seven from the book of Daniel which read: "The fourth beast will be a fourth kingdom [empire] on the earth, which will be different from all other kingdoms, and it will devour the whole earth and tread it down and crush it. As for the ten horns, out of this kingdom ten kings will arise and another will arise after them, and he will be different from the previous ones and will subdue three kings."

Also, Revelation 13:1 treats the same subject, "And I saw a beast coming up out of the sea, having ten horns and seven heads, and on his horns were ten diadems, and on his heads were blasphemous names."

On 1894, Mother Mary gave a prophecy to two children from La Salette in southeastern France. A paragraph from that prophecy reads: "There will be wars up to the last war which will be waged by the ten kings of Anti-Christ. These kings [or rulers] will have a common policy, and will be the only ones who reign upon the earth. Before that happens there will be a time of false peace in the world, and men will think only of pleasure."

BROTHERS AND SISTERS ARE MARKED BY THE BEAST

2:20 "Frères et soeurs en divers lieux captifs/Se trouveront passer près du monarque/Les contempler ses rameaux attentifs/Déplaisant voir menton, front, nez, les marques."

Brothers and sisters, who are held captive in diverse places,
Will find themselves passing by the monarch
And being contemplated by his attentive branches.
It is displeasing to see them being marked on their chins, foreheads and noses.

Brothers and sisters are Jews or Christians who are taken captive in diverse places and brought before the Anti-Christ **(the monarch)** whose followers **(branches)** will be watching them attentively while a mark of ownership is stamped on their faces. This mark of the AntiChrist is mentioned also in Revelation 13:16, "And he causes all, the small and the great, and the rich and the poor, and the free and the slave, to be given a mark on their right hand, or on their forehead."

A GREAT PRESCRIPTION IN ASIA

3:60 "Par toute Asie grande proscription/Même en Mysie, Lysie, et Pamphilie/Sang versera par absolution/D'un jeune noir rempli de félonie."

Through all Asia there will be a great proscription,
Even in Mysia, Lydia, and Pamphilla
Blood will be spilled because of the debauchery
Of a dark young man filled with felonies.

Mysia is the name of an ancient country in northwestern Asia Minor. **Lydia** is the name for another ancient country in the western of Asia Minor. **Pamphilia** is the name of an ancient district in southern Asia Minor. Presently Asia Minor forms the greater part of modern Turkey.

The **great prescription** refers to a dictatorship. Nostradamus is predicting the rise in power in Turkey of a leader whom he referred to as "a dark man filled with felonies" who will stir up the expansionist, religious, militarist, and warlike nature and ambitions of the Turks. It is expected that Nationalists and Islamists will take political power in Turkey and force Turkey to break its ties to the West.

THE COMING OF THE FLOODS

8: 16 "Au lieu que Hieron fait la nef fabriquer/Si grand déluge sera et si subite/Qu'on n'aura lieu ni terre s'attaquer/L'onde monter Fesulan Olympique."

At the place where Hieron had the ship built,
All of a sudden there will be a flood so great
That there will be neither spot nor land to set upon.
The waves are going even to mount the Fesulan olympic.

Hieron was an Italian leader who, at the time of the Etruscans, conquered Sicily and built temples there. Hence, the **place** in the first line is Etruria, the ancient country of the Etruscans, in central Italy. Hieron could not have invaded Sicily without ships. Also, the **ship** in the first line could refer to the temples he built in Sicily.

Ancient Faesulae (Fiesole) was one of the chief cities of the Etruscan confederacy, **Fesulan Olympic** refers to mainland Italy in his quatrain. (Olympic being the mountain abode of the gods in Greek mythology.)

The Etruscans probably migrated to Italy from Asia Minor c.900 B.C., their chief confederation included 12 cities. They traded extensively with the Greeks and Phoenicians and built up a civilization c. 500 B.C. At its peak Etruscan power extended into north Italy.

Also **floods** figuratively means human upheaval, riot, and war. A good example for that is psalm 93:3, "The floods have lifted up, O Lord, the floods have lifted up their voices; the floods lift up their pounding waves."

THE DEATH OF THE ANTI-CHRIST AND THE END OF WAR

1:100 "Longtemps au ciel sera vu gris oiseau/Aupres de Dole et de Toscane terre/Tenant au bec un verdoyant rameau/Mourra tot grand et finira la gueree."

For a long time a gray bird will be seen in the sky
Near Dole and the land of Tuscany,
Holding in its beak a green sprig.
The great one will die soon and the war will end.

The story of the bird with a green sprig in its beak is from the Bible. Genesis 8:11 reads, "And the dove came to him toward evening; and behold, in her beak was a freshly picked olive leaf. So Noah knew that the water was abated from the earth."

The cause of the would be flood is likely from the shifting of the poles of earth. Nostradamus, in his Epistle to the King, states: "And it will be in the month of October that some great dislocation [of the poles] will transpire and it will be such that one will think the mass of the earth has lost its natural movement." Such a shift is surely to cause great flooding, putting an end to the life of the Anti-Christ and destroying his mighty army, sometime near the year 2030.

Dole is a mountain peak in western Switzerland.

The Anti-Christ Deceives the Last Pope

8:4

The Cock [= the Arab Anti-Christ] will be received inside Monaco.

The Cardinal of France [= the last pope] will appear.

By persuasive dialogue the Roman [= the last pope] will be deceived.

Weakness for the Eagle [= the last pope] and power for the Cock will develop.

The Catholic Church is Destroyed

5:73

The Church of God will be persecuted,

And the holy Temples will be plundered.

[Both] the child and the mother, he [= the Arab Anti-Christ] will put naked in the nightgown [= he will put them to sleep of death].

The Arabs will be allied/joined with the Poles.

The Anti-Christ is Destroyed

5:68

[Paraphrased:] The great Camel [= the Arab Anti-Christ] will reach river Danube in Europe. Not willing to turn back he will get ready to advance toward the north—toward river Rhine. Tremble ye France [Rhone and Loire] because he will march toward you. It is near the Alps mountains that the Cock [the Anti-Christ] will be destroyed.

• • •

In the occult tradition the (false) Savior of the World is depicted as a muscular man with the head of a cock.

"Children on milk are dashed and bruised against the walls", page 56

A Roman Mosaic of Poseidon
Page 64

"Italy will become the play-ball of war. On every side blood will flow. The temples will either be closed or desecrated. Priests and members of religious orders will be put to flight. They will be beaten to death and otherwise die cruel deaths" (from La Salette prophecy of Mother Mary).

THE FIRE IS TO SPILL BLOOD, (C.6, Q.38). NO MERCY WILL BE SHOWN TO THE HUNGRY AND NAKED ONES, (C.6, Q.81). Page 65

Chapter 4

THE WAR IN ITALY

• • • • • • • • • • • •

HORRIBLE DAYS TO COME UPON THE ROMANS

2:30 "Un qui les dieux d'Annibal infernaux/Fera renaître, effrayeur des humains/Onc plus d'horreur ni plus pire journaux/Qu'avint viendra par Babel aux Romains."

One to whom the infernal gods of Hannibal
Will cause to be reborn - the terror of mankind.
Never more horrible nor worse days
Had come nor will ever come upon the Romans through Babylon.

Hannibal was a brilliant Carthaginian general who almost defeated Rome in the Second Punic War, B.C.
The **Romans** in line four are the present day Italians. And **Babylon** is the coming Arab empire.
This quatrain implies that the scourges of Hannibal were nothing compared to what is in store for Italy from the coming Arab Anti-Christ who will be the terror of mankind.

BATTLES AT SEA

5:62 "Sur les rochers sang on vera pleuvoir/Sol Orient, Saturne Occidental/Près d'Orgon querre, à Rome grand mal voir/Nefs parfondrées, et pris le Tridental."

Blood is seen washed on the rocks [of the shores].
Sun in the East, Saturn in the West.
Near Orgon war, at Rome great evil is seen.
Ships are sunk, and the Tridental is taken.

Sun in the Orient means success and victory for the oriental forces. **Saturn in Occidental** means misfortune and defeat for the western forces.

Orgon is a small town in southern France. In this quatrain it stands for the South of France.

Trident is a symbol of naval power. In ancient times, Poseidon, the god of the seas, was represented wielding a trident by which he provoked storms, set fire to the rocks, and caused springs to gush up. Thence Tridental became a symbol of naval forces.

ITALY DEFEATED AT LAND AND SEA

5:63 "De vaine emprinse l'honneur indue plainte/Galiotes errants par latins, froid, faim, vagues/Non loin du Tymbre de sang la terre teinte/ Et sur humains seront diverses plagues."

From the vain enterprise the honor is lamented unduly.
Erratic galleys are piloted, amid billows, by cold and hungry Italians.
Not far from the Tiber, the land is stained with blood,
And diverse plagues are come upon human beings.

Tiber is a river in central Italy; 252 miles (405 Km.) long. It rises in the Tuscan Apennines, flows south, in Latium turns southwest and flows through Rome which is 16 miles from its mouth at Ostia on the Tyrrhenian Sea.

Plagues in line four could refer to nuclear fallout and to the effects of biological and chemical weapons.

This quatrain implies Italy under attack and her consequent defeat by sea and land.

CARNAGE AND HELL IN THE MEDITERRANEAN AND IN ITALY

7:6 "Naples, Palerme, et toute la Sicille/Par main Barbare sera inhabitée/Corsique, Salterne, et de Sardeigne l'Ìsle/Faim, peste, guerre, fin des maux intentée."

Naples, Palermo and all Sicily
Will be uninhabited by Barbarian hand.
In Corsica, Salerno, and the Island of Sardinia,
Famine, plague, war and extreme evils.

6:81 "Pleurs, cris et plaintes, hurlements, effrayeur/Coeur inhuman, cruel Roy, et transi/Leman les Îles de Gennes les majeurs/Sang épancher, frofaim à nul merci."

Tears, cries and wails. Howling, terror.
The inhuman heart of a cruel and cold King.
Lake of Geneva, the Islands, the notables of Genoa,
Blood is spilled and no mercy is shown to the hungry and naked ones.

6:38 "Aux profligez de paix les ennemis/Après avoir l'Italie superée/ Noir sanguinaire rouge sera commis/Feu sang verser, eau de sang colorée."

The enemies of peace will act shamelessly and viciously
After having conquered Italy.
The bloody black one will be committed to red,
The fire is to spill blood, the water is to be colored by blood.

In the preceding quatrains, the **Barbarian hand**, the **cruel and cold King**, the **bloody black one** all are allusions to the Third Anti-Christ from the Middle East.

THE CITY OF ROME IS BURNED BY FIRE FROM THE SKY

2:81 "Part feu du ciel la cité presque aduste/L'Urne menece encore Deucalion/Vexée Sardaigne par la Punique fuste/Après que Libra lairra son Phaeton."

The city is almost burned down by fire from the sky.
The waters once more are threatening Deucalion.
Sardinia is vexed by the Punic fleet.
After that Libra will leave its Phaethon.

The **city** that is burned by airplane and missile firepower is Rome, Italy.
Deucalion was a Greek mythical character who survived a great flood. Line two is the implication of a deluge threatening areas of Italy.

Sardinia is an island west of the southern Italian peninsula. Together with some minor islands they constistute an autonomous region of Italy. The **Punic fleet** is that of the enemies of Italy.

Phaethon was the youth who in Greek mythology, while driving the solar chariot, lost control of the horses and caused the chariot to careen wildly through the sky and come close to Earth almost burning it up. Libra (a symbol of Balance and Justice) in this quatrain symbolizes the falling of the Sun, and the phrase **Libra will leave its Phaethon** signifies "a darkness will fall out at day time," which is a clear allusion to a solar eclipse. The first total solar eclipse for central Europe since 1961 is to occur on August 11, 1999. Its path: From the western Atlantic off Nova Scotia to the Scilly Isles and the southwest tip of Great Britain; through central Europe, the Middle East, India, and Pakistan, in the Bay of Bengal.

If the astrological interpretation of line four is correct, then the events depicted in lines 1, 2, and 3 are to occur before August 1999.

Immanuel Velikovsky, the author of "Worlds in Collision," also claims that the original conflagration of Phaethon occurred sometime near 1500 B.C., as a result of a comet coming very close to earth or "by a shifting of bodies in the sky which move around the earth." Velikovsky wrote: "The Greeks as well as the Carians and other people on the shores of the Aegean Sea told of a time when the sun was driven off its course and disappeared for an entire day, and the earth was burned and drowned. The Greek legend says that young Phaeton (the blazing star), who claimed parentage of the sun, on that fatal day tried to drive the chariot of the sun. Phaethon was unable to make his way 'against the whirling poles,' and 'the swift axis' swept him away."

Velikovsky quoted the Latin poet Ovid who told the story of Phaethon: "The earth bursts into flame, the highest parts first, and splits into deep cracks, and its moisture is all dried up. The meadows are burned to white ashes; the trees are consumed, green leaves and all, and the ripe grain furnishes fuel for its own destruction....Great cities perish with their walls, and the vast conflagration reduces whole nations to ashes."

Ovid also wrote (in his **Metamorphoses**, Book II) that the chariot of the sun, driven by Phaethon, moved "no longer in the same course as before," the horses "break loose from their course," and "if we are to believe report, one whole day went without the sun. But the burning world gave light." Then Ovid ends his description of the Conflagration of Phaethon: "Causing all things to shake with her mighty trembling, she sank back a little lower than her wonted place." Apparently, the earth changed the inclination of its axis.

Velikovsky raises the question: "How could the poets have know that a change in the movement of the sun across the firmament must cause a world conflagration, blazing of volcanoes, boiling of rivers, disappearance of seas, birth of deserts, emergence of islands, if the sun never changed its harmonious journey from sunrise to sunset?" (Worlds in Collision, Chapter 7).

Velikovsky also writes that "the flood of Deucalion is described by Greek authors as having been simultaneous with the conflagration of Phaethon....the flood brought overwhelming destruction to the mainland of Greece and the islands around and caused changes in the geographical profile of the area....water covered the land and annihilated the population. According to the legend, only two persons, Deucalion and his wife, remained alive."

ITALY THE GREAT IS LAID TO WASTE

3:33 "En la cité où le loup entrera/Bien près de là les ennemis seront/ Copie étrange grand pays gâtera/Aux murs et Alpes les amis passeront."

The city where the wolf will enter in,
Near by the enemies will be.
A foreign army will lay a great country to waste.
The friends will come crossing the barriers of the Alps.

The **wolf** is the last pope who will betray the Catholic Church. The **city** is Rome under siege by armies of the Arab Anti-Christ. A **great country** that is laid to waste is Italy. The **friends** crossing the Alps mountains and liberating Italy are the French and her allies under the command of "Ogmios," the great Celt.

THE FRENCH ARMY ENTERS DEEP INTO ITALY

4:37 "Gaulois par sauts, monts viendra pénétrer/Occupera le grand lieu de l'Insubre/Au plus profond son ost fera entrer/Gennes, Monech pousseront classe rubre."

The Frenchman will penetrate the mountains by leaps
And occupy the great area of Milan.

He will lead his army deeper in the land.
Genoa and Monaco will hurl away the red fleet.

THE GREAT CELT ENTERS ROME

6:28 "Le grand Celtique entrera dedans Rome/menant amas d'exilés et bannis/Le grand Pasteur mettra à mort tout homme/Qui pour le coq étaient aux Alpes unis."

The great Celt will enter Rome,
Bringing the exiled and banished back.
The great pastor will put to death all men
Who were united with the Cock at the Alps.

The **Frenchman** (the Gaul), **Ogmios**, the **great Celt** and the **great pastor** all are the same person; a French hero who will defeat the forces of the Arab Anti-Christ. The **Cock** in line four is the Anti-Christ.

THE RED ONES DRIVEN OUT OF ITALY

9:2 "De haut du mont Aventin, voix ouie/Videz, videz de tous les deux cotés/Du sang des rouges sera l'ire assomie/D'Arimin Prato, Columna debotez."

A voice is heard from the top of mount Aventine,
"Come down, come down all the way, from both sides."
The wrath will be appeased by shedding the blood of the red ones
Who are driven out from Rimini, Prato and Colonne.

Mount Aventine is one of the seven hills of Rome. In early times, the hills—which are of volcanic origin—were very abrupt. In ancient times, the Plebeians when vexed by the Patrician tyranny withdrew and took refuge in mount Aventine. The first two lines imply that the forces of the Anti-Christ are in retreat and the call of attack and pursuit is heard in Italy.

The **red ones** are the forces of the Anti-Christ.

Rimini (ancient Ariminum) is a seaport in northern Italy on the Adriatic, and was a Roman military base in the Second Punic War and during the Gothic invasions. **Prato** is a commune in Tuscany, west Italy. **Colonne Cape** is a cape on the east coast of Calabria, southern Italy.

OGMIOS WILL RAISE HIS ENSIGN THROUGHOUT ITALY

6:42 "A Logmion sera laisee le regne/Du grand selin, qui plus fera de fait/Par les Itales etendra son enseigne/Regi sera par prudent contrefait."

To Ogmios will be left the realm
Of the great Selin, who will do more exploits:
Throughout Italy he will raise his ensign,
He will be governed by prudent deformity.

In Mythology, **Ogmios** is the Celtic Hercules. The Celts (i.e. the French) portrayed him as a very old man, with a bald head, save at the back of his head, where his remaining hair is completely white. His skin was coarse and wrinkled and his tongue pierced (hence, the reference to deformity in line four). He was the eloquence who was the symbol of the power of the ritual word which united the world of men with the world of the gods. It was his name that was offered in blessings for one's friends and curses against one's enemies. In this quatrain, **Ogmios** refers to a Christian hero who will do more exploits than the Arab Anti-Christ who is referred to by Selin. **Selin** or selene are names for the moon; the crescent moon is an emblem of Islam.

"This Awareness indicates there is seen validity in this attempt [of Galileo] to create a sun out of Jupiter. The real purpose being to heat Mars to make it habitable; to create an atmosphere with the new sun and certain other activities directed to Mars, to make it habitable for life forms and for vegetation.

"There are certain activities that must occur on Mars to create the atmosphere needed. The atmosphere would also need a sun to be closer. The sun of your solar system, over periods of time, is gradually becoming smaller and those planets further out are not receiving enough heat to allow them to become habitable without assistance.

"Thus, the concept of creating a sun out of Jupiter (even though the sun would be quite small in size), that concept of creating that extra heat for Mars would solve the problem. The problem, however, might be shifted to Earth, where the polar caps will melt and raise water levels, flooding many of the shoreline cities and diminishing the land mass considerably and possibly creating a heating of the Earth, making it more difficult to inhabit. (The Reptoids and Zetas enjoy the heat and would benefit from such event—the binary sun increasing the temperature on Earth). Humans would need to have a cooler place to live. These things have been studied carefully and many scientists are working on this concept of creating two other living planets (Mars and Venus) for humanity."

Cosmic Awareness

THE APPEARANCE OF TWO SUNS

2:41 "Le grande étoile par sept jours brûlera/Nuée fera deux soleils apparoir/Le gros mâstin toute nuite hurlera/Quand grand pontife chang-era de terroir."

The great star will scorch for seven days.
Cloud will cause two suns to appear.
The dark-blue mastiff will howl all night.
While the great pontiff will change his abode.

The **great star** is our sun. It is great if compared to Jupiter which is an un-ignited small sun. Both are made mostly of hydrogen and helium. **Seven days** are one week (7 years); a jubilee = 49 years = 7 weeks.

Cloud is a Biblical term for spaceship. There is a secret U.S. govern-ment and certain of Zeta-Retuculi-Greys joint project of creating a sun out of planet Jupiter.

According to this quatrain of Nostradamus, the attempt will be suc-cessful, unfortunately it will have adverse effects on earth, causing dan-gerous weather patterns; the heat parching and scorching our planet.

According to Cosmic Awareness "Element 115 is an alien element brought to earth by extraterrestrials. It is thousands of times more potent than plutonium and the nuclear energy found on earth" (R. of A., 1994–7, page 13).

Cosmic Awareness has indicated that "indeed, it is possible that a second sun could be created [out of Jupiter] if certain energies and places impact simultaneously in a particular order" (R. of A., 1994-10, page 2).

The **dark-blue mastiff** could be a reference to planet earth or to the Third Anti-Christ who will remain sleepless.

The **great pontiff** who will be forced to change his residency from Vatican to another land is the penultimate or the last pope. (See also sextet No. 30, page 77).

Cloud is also an indication of the divine presence of God both in the Old and New Testaments. And the **two suns** could be two popes.

Also, the first two lines of this quatrain has been interpreted as a close encounter of a comet with earth.

• • • • • •

John Paul II

Chapter 5

THE PAPACY IN PROPHECY

"We were told that the present pope, John Paul II, would be assassinated while on one of his trips, (presumably in the spring in a large city in Europe that sat near the juncture of two major rivers.) After his death another pope would be elected who would only serve for a short time because he would be assassinated (by poison) by those within the Church....After this, a pope would be elected who conformed more to their wishes, but who would prove to be the tool of the coming Anti-Christ. Through their association, the downfall of the Catholic Church would be accomplished."

Dolores Cannon

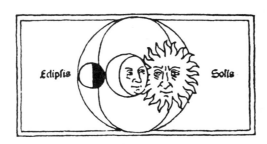

"You must pray for your Holy Father, the Pope. There will be another attempt upon his life. Yes, My child, though he means well, it would be best if he discards his habit of going to and fro. For it is upon one of these journeys that he will be destroyed."

Our Lady, May 17, 1986

"My child and My children, you will continue to pray for your Vicar in Rome, Pope John Paul II. At this very moment, there is now being held a conference in secret to the world for his extermination, and to place upon the Seat of Peter the despot."

Our Lady, October 6, 1992

OUR LADY OF THE ROSES SHRINE
P.O. Box 52 • Bayside, NY 11361

THE ELECTION OF JOHN PAUL II

5:92 "Après le siége tenu dix-sept ans/Cinq changeront en tel révolu terme/Puis sera l'un élu de même temps/Qui des Romains ne sera trop conforme."

After the See has been held for 17 years [by Pius XII],
Five will change within the same period of time.
Then one [=John Paul II] will be elected at that time,
Who will bear little resemblance to the Romans.

Pope Pius XII died after a term of 19 years in October, 1959. Hence there is a mistake of two years.

In the years from October 1959 to October 1978 (during a total of 19 years) there were five pontiffs.

The distinctly non-Roman Polish Cardinal Karol Wojtyla was elected pontiff in the year 1978. Nostradamus hints in this quatrain that his reign will last for 19 years.

Nostradamus code-named John Paul II (who was born during a solar eclipse) as the "Sun." In C.3, Q.34 he predicts his death:

When the default of the Sun takes place,
The monster [=the Arab Anti-Christ] will be seen in broad daylight;
Though, at the time, it will be interpreted otherwise.
The High Price [=the Pope] left unguarded, no one could have fore-
seen it [=his assassination].

THE DEATH Of PAUL MENSOLE

8:46 "Pol mensolee mourra trois lieues du Rosne/Fuis les deux prochains tarasc destrois/Car Mars fera le plus horrible trone/De coq et d'aigle de France freres trois."

Paul Mensole will die at three leagues from Rosne.
His two immediate successors are put to flight by the Monster of Tarascon.

For the horrible reigning Mars will make of itself,
Of the Cock, and the Eagle of France three bedfellows.

This quatrain refers to Pope John Paul II **(Paul Mensole)** and his death at a distance of three leagues from Rosne (**Rosne** being a possible anagram for Rosny). It also refers to his next two successors who would be persecuted by the **Monster of Tarascon** (i.e. the Antichrist) and eventually destroyed. It will be a time of trouble and of wars (i.e. **Mars**), involving among others France and the Arab Anti-Christ (**the Cock**).

St. Malachy, the Catholic saint of twelfth century, gave the following mottos to the three last popes: "De Labore Solis" (Latin for the work of the sun) to Pope John Paul II. "De Gloria Olivae" (Latin for—of the glory of the olive tree) to the penultimate pope, implying that he will be faithful to the Church. "Petrus Romanus" to his successor and the last pope. It is Latin for Peter the Roman.

Nostradamus referred to Pope John Paul II by the motto: "Pol Mensole," Pol is Latin for Paul; Sol is Latin for sun, Manus is Latin for "man's work, travail, industry, labor," an overall accurate description of Pope John Paul II

Tarascon is a French town that is associated with a legendary monster "La Tarasque" which is said to have ravaged that area. Nostradamus used it as a symbol for the Anti-Christ.

Rosny-sur-Seine is a small commune near Paris, France.

Mars is the god of war in mythological lore.

The "**Eagle of France**" is the French last pope from France.

THE LAST THREE POPES

2:57: "Avant conflit le grand mur tombera/Le grand a mort, mort trop subite et plainte/Ne imparfait: la plupart nagera/Aupres du fleuve de sang la terre teinte."

Before the conflict the great wall will fall.
The great one will die a hasty and lamented death.
Born imperfect, he will swim most of the time
By the river, while the earth will be tainted with blood.

The **great wall** in the first line is Pope John Paul II, Nostradamus referred to him by the wall because of his immovable conservatism. He will die before the war (**conflict**) commences.

His successor who is referred to as **the great one** will die unexpectedly and be lamented.

The last Pope, who is born with a physical defect, will survive (**swim by the river of life**) while the earth will be tainted with blood due to a great war.

THE PENULTIMATE POPE

2:28 "Le pénultième du surnom du prophète/Prendra Diane pour son jour et repos/Loin vaguera par frénétique tête/Et délivrant un grand peuple d'impos."

The penultimate of surname of the prophet,
Will take Diana for his day and rest.
He will be far from idleness because of his zeal,
In delivering a great people from subjugation.

The **penultimate** in the first line is the penultimate pope who will act like goddess Diana while active by day and while at rest in night. The warrior-hunter goddess Diana had no time for trifles. She was there when needed. **Diana Victorious**, and her brother Apollo, were considered to be the protectors of Imperial Rome and guarantors of peace imposed by the Roman Empire.

The **great people** whom the Pope will work hard to deliver from falling under the control of the Arab Anti-Christ are the faithful Catholics of Italy and Europe.

[Note: **Vaquera** in the French verse is the future tense of **vaquer** an old form of saying "to be vacant, to be idle."]

THE SHORT TENTURE OF THE PENULTIMATE POPE

8:93 "Sept mois sans plus obtiendra prélature/Par son décès grand schisme fera naître/Sept mois tiendra un autre la préture/Près de Venise paix, union renaître."

He will acquire the prelacy only for seven months.
Because of his death a great schism will arise.
For seven months another will hoid the praetorship.
Near Venice peace and union is reestablished.

Prelacy is the office or rank of a prelate, a high ranking ecclesiastic. **Praetor** was the name given to a magistrate of ancient Rome, he was next below a consul in rank. **Venice** is a famous seaport in northeastern Italy.

This quatrain, most likely, is an allusion to the penultimate pope and the schism that will arise in the Catholic hierarchy following his unexpected death.

THE DEATH OF THE PENULTIMATE POPE

Sextet 30
Dans peu de temps Medecin du grand mal,
Et la sangsuë d'order et rang inegal,
Mettront le feu à la branche d'Olive,
Poste courir, d'un et d'autre coste,
Et par tel feu leur Empire accoste,
Se r'alumant du franc finy salive.

In a short time the Physician of great evil,
And the leech of unequal order and rank,
Will put the Olive Branch on fire.
[His] post will be moved from one coast to another,
And by so great fire their Empire will be accosted
That the heat will evaporate the saliva in the mouth.

The first three lines refer to the poisoning of the penultimate pope, known as the **Olive Branch or Tree**, and his being visited by fever (**fire**) by his enemies. Incidentally, in Medieval times the leech was used to suck the blood of the sick; Nostradamus the physician, knowing the role played by the blood in healing, refused to use the blood-sucking methods of medical profession of his days.

The **post** in line four refers to the papal see.

The **fire** and **heat** mentioned in lines five and six could either be the result of war or the close passing of a comet.

THE LAST POPE TO DISHONOR THE PAPAL SEE

5:56 "Par le trepas du tres vieillard Pontife/Sera elu Romain de bon age/Qui sera dit que le siege debiffe/Et long tiendra, et de piquant ouvrage."

Through the death of the very old Pontiff
The Roman of good age will be elected.
Of him it will be said he dishonors the see,
And he will sit long and his deeds will sting.

The **very old Pontiff** in the first line is the penultimate pope. The **Roman of good age** is the last pope who is labeled by St. Malachy (1094-1148) as "Peter the Roman." St. Malachy commented on him thus: "Peter the Roman will sit upon the papal throne in time of extreme persecution of the holy Roman Church. He will pasture the sheep midst multiple tribulations, during which the city of seven hills [Rome] will be destroyed and the powerful Judge [God] will judge the populace."

St. Francis of Assisi also could have been referring to the last pope when he stated: "There will be an uncanonically elected pope who will cause a great schism, there will be divers thoughts preached which will cause many to agree with those heretics which will cause even my order to divide, then will there be such universal dissensions and persecutions that if these days were not shortened even the elect would be lost."

THE LAST POPE TO BECOME WOLFISH

8:31 "Premier grand fruit le Prince de Pesquiere/Mais puis viendra bien et cruel malin/Dedans Venise perdra sa gloire fière/Et mis à mal par plus juene Celin."

First great fruits of the Prince of the fishermen,
But then his very cruel evils will come.
He will lose his precious glory in Venice,
And be made to fall by the more youthful Selin.

This quatrain refers to the last pope who at first will manifest the good deeds of the Apostle Peter (**the Prince of the fishermen**). However, soon he will become wolfish and do evil.

The **youthful Selin** in line four is the Arab Anti-Christ, the crescent moon being an indication of the Moslem world. **Selin** is a mythical name for the moon.

THE DEATH OF THE LAST POPE

2:97 "Romain Pontife garde de t'approcher/De la cite que deux fleuves arrose/Ton sang viendra auprès de là cracher/Toi et les tiens quand fleurira la rose.

Roman Pontiff beware of approaching
The city that two rivers run through.
Near there your blood will spill;
Yours and that of your retinue, when the rose blooms.

The **Roman Pontiff** in the first line is the last pope who, along with his entourage, would be in danger to being killed—in late Spring when the roses bloom—while approaching a city that two rivers flow through.

Also, this quatrain may refer to the assassination of pope Paul John II while celebrating the "World Youth Day" in Paris, France, sometime in the year 1997. An alternate translation of the second line is—"The city that is watered (or irrigated) by two rivers." Actually, the city of Paris is watered or irrigated by two rivers: Marne and Seine.

The **Rose** is a symbol of Mother Mary. John Paul II has given himself totally to her. Also, the thriving of "the rose" refers to a place, like Paris, where culture and civilization is in bloom.

1997 is also the likely year when a new totalitarian regime in Russia would launch, from submarines, a first nuclear strike upon U.S.A., partially destroying our nation.

1997 is also the year when the Third Anti-Christ will be seen in broad daylight as he comes to power in Egypt. And after working for global peace for three years he will start the dreaded World War III.

THE LAST POPE IS BORN IN FRANCE

5:49 "Nul de l'espagne, mais de l'antigue France/Né, sera élu pour la tremblante nacelle./À l'ennemi sera faite fiancé/Qui dans son regne sera peste cruelle."

Not from Spain, but [the one] of the ancient France
Born, will be elected for the trembling wherry (gondola).
A "fiance" of the enemy he [the pope] will be;
Who [the enemy] in his [pope's] kingdom will be a cruel pest.

This quatrain clearly refers to the last pope who is born in France. The cardinal from Spain will not be elected pope.

The **trembling wherry** refers to the papal chair being in turmoil.

This last pope will be in league (secretly or openly) with the Arab Anti-Christ (= **the enemy**), who will prove to be a pest and acting like one will destroy the Catholic kingdom.

[6:86, which is not included in this book, suggests that the would be last pope is or has been the prelate (archbishop) of Sens, which is an historic city in the region of Yonne of France. Sens is an archiepiscopal see since 1817.]

THE INFERNAL PRINCE ENTERING THE SANCTUARY

A prophecy of Mother Mary, given in 1979, through Veronica Lueken, the seer of Bayside.

"My Children, it is a delusion for mankind to believe that a form and manner of humanism shall save the world. Modernism shall destroy the world and my Son's Church; but not the foundation, for my Son is the foundation. Though the walls may crumble, the pillars may shake, the foundation is solid; for it is My Son, and it shall be rebuilt, after the great Chastisement, to its former glory. The Eternal Father has full control over your world; though, in your free will now, He will allow you to follow your own course to destruction."

THE CATHOLIC CHURCH IS RETURNED TO A RENOWNED PRESTIGE

5:74 "De sang Troyen naîtra coeur Germanique/Qui deviendra en si haute puissance/Hors chassera étrange Arabique/Tournant l'Eglise en pristine prééminence."

A Germanic heart born of Trojan blood
Will attain to so great a power,
He will drive out the foreign Arabs,
Returning the Church to a renowned prestige.

Legend has it that the French rulers are descendents of Francus, son of Priam of Troy. Hence the **Trojan blood** refers to a French ruler. **Germanic**, or the Latin Germanicus meaning "of the Germans," was originally applied to a particular tribe, probably Celtic.

This quatrain could be an allusion to Ogmios, the French hero who will defeat the Moslem forces of the Arab Anti-Christ. The **Church** in line four is the Catholic Church, of course, administered from the Vatican.

"In an instant a great scattered flame will leap up, /When they will want to give the Normans a proof of their might" (C.6, Q.97). Page 89.

Chapter 6

THE WAR IN FRANCE, GERMANY AND SWITZERLAND

• • • • • • • • • • • • • • • •

THE ANTI-CHRIST INVADES SOUTH FRANCE

3:62 "Proche del duero par mer Tyrrene close/Viendra percer les grands monts Pyrénées/La main plus courte et sa perce glose/À Carcassonne conduira ses menees."

Toward the Douro, from the enclosure of Tyrrhenia
He will come in order to pierce the great Pyrenees mountains,
His hand too short and his advance being observed,
He will conduct his scheming to Carcassone.

This quatrain is about the Arab Anti-Christ whose fleet will be approaching Spain (**the river Douro**) from the region of the Tyrrhenian Sea, his strategy being to invade France by crossing the Pyrenees mountains from Spain. However, when he falls short of reinforcements (**his hand too short**) and his movements are discovered by the Spaniards, he will give up his original plan and instead assault south France (**Carcassone**) directly from the French shore.

Douro or Spanish Duero is a 556 miles long river in Spain and Portugal. **Tyrrhenian Sea** is the part of the Mediterranean Sea west of the Italian mainland, north of Sicily, and east of Sardinia and Corsica. **Carcassone** is a French town north of the Pyrenees. The **Pyrenees** is a mountain range along the French-Spanish border.

A GREAT ARMY BY SEA TO APPROACH MARSEILLE

3:88 "De Barselonne par mer si grande armée/Toute Marseille de frayeur tremblera/Îles saisies de mer aide fermée/Ton traditeur en terre nagera."

**From Barcelona so great an army by sea,
All Marseille will tremble with fear.
The Isles are seized, from sea the help is shut off.
Your traitor will swim on land.**

Barcelona is an important Catalonia seaport in northeastern Spain. **Marseille** is a major commercial French seaport on the northeastern shore of the Gulf of Lion. It is also a military and naval station. The **Isles** are islands in the eastern Mediterranean Sea.

The **great army by sea** in the first line is the fleet of the Arab Anti-Christ who, after aborting his assault on Barcelona, will turn around and invade instead south France, causing the inhabitants of Marseille to tremble from fear.

Your traitor in line four refers to the traitor of France who will invade its lands. Apparently the Anti-Christ will break his non-belligerent and friendship treaty with France.

A WARNING TO THE FRENCH FLEET

3:87 "Classe Gauloise n'approches de Corseigne/Moins de Sardaigne, tu t'en repentiras/Trestous mourrez frustrés de l'aide Grogne/ Sang nagera captif ne me croiras."

**French fleet, do not approach to Corsica,
Even less to Sardinia, otherwise you will regret it:
All of you will die cut off of aid from the mainland;
You would not believe me if I told you that you'll swim in blood and be taken prisoners.**

A WORD OF ADVICE TO THE FRENCH FORCES

3:23 "Si France passes outre mer Lygustique/Tu te verras en îles et mers enclose/Mahommet contraire: plus mer hadriatique/Chevaux et d'ânes tu rongeras les os."

If the French forces pass beyond the Liqurian Sea,
They will find themselves fenced in by the islands and seas:
Muhammad and the Adriatic Sea opposite of them:
They will gnaw the bones of horses and donkeys.

Liqurian Sea is a branch of the Mediterranean Sea enclosed by the Italian regions of Liguira and Tuscany, north and east, and the French island of Corsica on the south; this area includes the Gulf of Genoa.

The **Adriatic Sea** is an arm of the Mediterranean Sea between Italy and the Balkan peninsula; about 500 miles long, with an average width of about 110 miles.

Muhammad in this quatrain indicates the Moslem forces. The "eating of the bones of horses and donkeys" refers to the utter destruction and defeat of Moslem forces by the French - provided they follow the advice of Nostradamus.

FRANCE DEFEATED BECAUSE OF DISCORD AND NEGLIGENCE

1:18 "Par la discorde négligence Gauloise/Sera passage à Mahomet ouvert/De sang trempé le terre et mer Senoise/Le port Phocen de voiles et nefs couvert."

Because of the French discord and negligence
A passage to Muhammad is made open:
The land and sea of Siena are soaked in blood,
The Phocaean port is covered with sails and ships.

Muhammad in line two refers to the invading Moslem forces who gain access (**passage**) to Italy (**Siena**) and south France (**Marselle**) because of French discord and negligence.

Siena is a province in Tuscany, in western Italy. The **Phocaean port** in line four is the city of Marseille which was originally founded in B.C. by Phocaea, an ancient city on Aegean Sea, and an important maritime state c. 100-600 B.C., one of the first to engage in voyages of discovery.

FRANCE ASSAILED FROM FIVE SIDES

1:73 "France à cinq parts par neglect assaillie/Tunis, Argiels émus par Persiens/Leon, Seville, Barcelona faillie/N'aura la classe par les Venitiens."

France due to negligence is assailed from five sides.
Tunisia, Algeria are stirred by Persians.
Leon, Sevilla, and Barcelona are in decline.
The Venetians will lack the fleet.

Tunisia and **Algeria** are two African Arab nations. **Persians** are the modern Iranians. **Leon, Sevilla, and Barcelona** are three Spanish cities. The **Venetians** are the Italians.

MARSEILLE DEVASTATED

10:88 "Pieds et Cheval à la seconde veille/Feront entrée vastient tout par la mer/Dedans le poil entrera de Marseille/Pleurs, cris, et sang, onc nul temps si amer."

Foot and horse at the second watch.
They will make an entry from the sea, devastating all.
He will enter into the nakedness of Marseilles.
Tears, cries, and blood; never times so sorrowful.

Watch is a measure of time unto which the 12 hours of the night were divided. The ancient Romans divided it into four watches; while the Hebrew division was threefold. **Foot and horses** refers to the enemy army observed or heard by the watchmen.

La poil in the French verse is a slang word which could mean either: hair or being naked. Marseille being naked indicates her helplessness, and the one who will enter into her is the Arab Anti-Christ or one of his commanders.

THE EVACUATION OF MARSEILLE

1:72 "Du tout Marseille des habitants changée/Course et poursuite jusqu'auprès de Lyon/Narbonne, Tholouse par Bourdeaux outragée/ Tués captifs presque d'un million."

Marseille is evacuated of its inhabitants;
Who are put to flight and pursued almost to Lyons.
Narbonne, Toulouse are outraged from the direction of Bordeaux.
Killed and captive nearly a million.

Lyons is a city in eastern France, at the confluence of the Rhone and Saone rivers. **Narbonne** is a town near the Mediterranean Sea, thirty one miles east of Carcassone. **Toulouse** is a city located just north of Carcassone. **Bordeaux** is a commercial seaport and industrial city at the Bay of Biscay, France.

THE DEVASTATION OF THE FRENCH RIVIERA

3:82 "Freins, Antibol, villes autour de Nice/Seront vastées fer, par mer at par terre/Les sauterelles terre et mer vent propice/Pris, morts, troussés, pillés sans loi de guerre."

Frejus, Antibe, towns around Nice,
Will be devastated by sword, from sea and land:
The wind being propitious, the locusts are on land and sea,
Captured, killed, bound, pillaged without regard to laws of war.

Nice is an historical region in southeastern France. The main city Nice is a seaport and leading resort city of the French Riviera. **Frejus** is a town in southeastern France. **Antibe** is a seaport in southeastern France, eleven miles southwest of Nice.

Sword in line two refers to war. The **locusts** in line three indicate the people of north Africa. The locusts originate from Africa, sometimes they get carried along by the hot winds of the African desert all the way to South Europe.

This quatrain is about a great devasation coming upon South France through war. The invading Moslem forces from Africa will go on a rampage of killing and looting without paying any consideration to laws and treaties governing the conduct of war.

MORE PILLAGE AND PLUNDER

2:4 "Depuis Monech jusqu'auprès de Sicille/Toute la plage demeurera désolée/IL n'y aura faubourg, cité, ni ville/Que par Barbares pillée soit et volée."

**From Monaco as far as Sicily
All the shores will remain desolated.
There will not be a suburb, city, nor town left
That is not pillaged and plundered by the Barbarians.**

Monaco is an independent principality on the Mediterranean Sea, near the French-Italian border, about 370 acres in area. **Sicily** is the largest island in the Mediterranean Sea, west of the extreme southern point of Italian peninsula. In the ninth century it was overrun by Moslems. The **Barbarians** in line four are the warring modern Moslem forces of the Arab Anti-Christ pillaging south Europe and making it desolate.

TOULOUSE UNDER ATTACK

9:46 "Videz, fuyez de Tolose les rouges/Du sacrifice faire expiation/ Le chef du mal dessous l'ombre des courges/Mort étrangler carne omination."

**Get out, flee from Toulouse. The reds
Will be swift in making sacrifices of you.
The greatest harm will fall below the shadow of the bombs;
What a strange death! The flesh is thrown off the bones.**

Toulouse is a city in southern France, a railroad junction and canal port. It is also a center of the French aviation industry.

The **courges** in the French verse means gourds, any of a group of vines including squash, pumpkin, and melon. Nostradamus used it in a figurative way to indicate bombs.

The fourth line could be a description of the effects of cobalt and nuclear bombs.

The **red ones** in line first are evidently the forces of the Anti-Christ who will make burnt sacrifices of the inhabitants of Toulouse.

FRANCE ATTACKED BY AN ATOMIC MISSILE

6:97 "Cinq et quarante degrés ciel brûlera/Feu approcher de la grande cité neuve/Instant grande flamme éparse sautera/Quand on voudra des Normans faire preuve."

At forty-five degrees the sky will burn,
Fire to approach the great new city.
In an instant a great scattered flame will leap up,
When they will want to give the Normans a proof of their might.

The 45 degrees north Latitude line crosses south France. The **great new city** in line two could be an allusion to the new Republic of France or to a southern French city. The sky burning and fire approaching the city could be the result of a launched missile.

The leaping scattered flame in line three is the mushroom-like dispersion of an atomic explosion. The **Normans** are the French.

AN ORIENTAL RULER COMES TO FRANCE

2:29 "L'Oriental sortira de son siège/Passer les monts Apennins, voir la Gaule/Transpercera du ciel les eaux et neige/Et un chacun frappera de sa gaule."

The Oriental leaving his headquarters
Will pass the Appenines mountains and come to France.
He will traverse the sky, the waters and the snow,
And in each will strike with his rod.

The **Oriental** in this quatrain refers to the Anti-Christ. The **Appenines** are a mountain range in central Italy, arbitrarily divided from the Ligurian Alps in the northwest of Italy, extending the full length of the peninsula in a bow-shaped range.

Lines three and four indicate that the forces of the Anti-Christ will traverse the air, the waters, and the snowy lands, leaving a trail of destruction and violence wherever they go, as stated by the prophet: "The land is like the garden of Eden before them, but a desolate wilderness behind them" (the book of Joel 2:3).

RUSSIA'S "LAST DASH" TO THE SOUTH AND TO WEST

5:54 "Du pont Euxine et la grand Tartarie/Un Roi sera qui viendra voir la Gaule/Transpercera Alane et l'Armenie/Et dans Bisance lairra sanglante gaule."

From the Black Sea and the great Tartary,
A would be king will come to see France.
He will transpire Alania and Armenia,
And in Byzantium will leave his bloody rod.

The **great Tartary** in this verse indicates the Russian Federation and her allies. Tartary or Tatary was a vast region in East Europe, Asia and Central Asia under the control of Tatar tribes in the late Middle Ages: Its greatest extent was from southwestern Russia to the Pacific.

In the Wall-Map of Europe (IMAGO MUNDI), Amsterdam 1595, the location of the great Tartary is put in northwest of Moscow, while the smaller Kingdom of Tartaria is put in southeast of Moscow.

Presently, Tartar or Tatarstan is an autonomous republic of Federated Russia, located in the eastern part at the bend of the Middle Volga, having an area of 36,255 sq. miles only. In 1552, Tatary was conquered by Moscow under Ivan the Terrible. In 1920, it was established as an autonomous republic. The Tartars are Mongolian and Turkish people.

The **king** in line two refers to a new Russian leader.

Alania is an ancient name for lands inhabited by the Alans, in north Caucasus and Armenia.

Armenia or biblical Minni is an ancient country in Western Asia, now divided between the Republic of Armenia (formerly the Armenia Soviet Socialist Republic of the USSR), Turkey, Iran, and Azerbaijan.

Byzantium is an ancient city, the site of modern Istanbul in Turkey. It was once known as Constantinople.

THE HOLY ROMAN EMPIRE IS REBORN

5:94 "Translatera en la grand Germanie/Brabant et Flandres, Gand, Bruges et Bolongne/La trefue feinte, le grand Duc d'Armenie/Assaillira Vienne et la Cologne."

It is to change into Greater Germany,
Brabant and Flanders, Ghent, Bruges and Bologna.
The truce is phony: The great Duke of Armenia

Will assail Vienna and Cologne.

The first two lines define the boundaries of the Holy Roman Empire in the twelve century. The Holy Roman Empire of west-central Europe comprised the German-speaking peoples and North Italy. It began in A.D. 800 with the papal crowning of Charlemage or, in an alternate view, with the crowning of Otto I in 962. It lasted until Francis II (who was Francis I of Austria) resigned the title in 1806.

The **Duke of Armenia** in line two refers to a Russian army commander of Armenian origin. **Vienna** is the capital of Austria. **Cologne** is a German city on the Rhine.

This quatrain implies that the Russians will assault the revived Holy Roman Empire (the European Union/NATO?) during World War III.

THE HOLY EMPIRE WILL COME TO GERMANY

10:31 "Le sainct Empire viendra en Germanie/Ismaëlites trouveront lieux ouverts/Âsnes voudront aussi la Carmanie/Les soustenant de terre tous couverts."

The holy Empire will come to Germany.
The Ishmaelites will find the sites open.
The donkeys shall want also Carmania.
The supporters are all covered by earth.

The **holy Empire** in the first line is Russia. The term "Holy Russia" arose as a reflection of the multitude of saints that inhabited Russia over the centuries and was invoked to inspire Russians to protect the sacred heritage of Orthodox Christianity. "Holy Russia" never meant that the country itself was sacred, or that all Russians were holy.

The **sites** in the second line are the holy sites in Jerusalem and the modern Israel. The **Ishmaelites** are the northern Arabs who are descendants from Ishmael, the son of the Patriarch Abraham from Hagar. The **donkeys** in line three are the Arabs or the Ishmaelites. They are often referred to by that name because the angel of the Lord told Hagar (in Genesis 16:12) that Ishmael "will be a wild donkey of a man."

Jesus demonstrated his love for the Arabs by specifically requesting a donkey from his followers to ride it into Jerusalem midst the shouts of Hosannas. Jesus was bringing a message of peace for two warring brothers; those descendants from Ishmael, and those descandants from Isaac. His message is as valid today as it was then.

Carmania is an ancient name for a region in modern Iran, near Pakistan. However, in this quatrain it refers to Asia Minor or modern Turkey. When Nostradamus penned this verse, Carmania was understood to be a region in Asia Minor; in the Wall-Map of Europe (IMAGO MUNDI), 1595, "Caramania" is put in Asia Minor, just west of ancient Cilicia.

The **supporter** in line four could refer to the allies of Germany, Israel and Turkey who are unable to help when those latter countries are invaded by the Russians and Arabs.

A SHORT LIVED PEACE TREATY

1:92 "Sous un la paix partout sera clamée/Mais non longtempe pille et rébellion/Par refus ville, terre et mer entamée/Mort et captifs le tiers d'un million."

The peace will be proclaimed everywhere by one,
But shortly afterwards pillage and rebellion.
Because of a refusal, town, earth and sea are invaded,
Dead and captives [number] one third of a million.

The one under whom peace will be acclaimed could be a world leader. The refusal in line three is about not surrendering or capitulating to this world leader.

ANTI-CHRIST TO REIGN IN AVIGNON

8:52 "Le Roi de Blois dans Avignon regner/D'Amboise et seme viendra le long de Lyndre/Ongle à Poitiers saintes ailes ruiner/Devant Boni."

The King of Blois to reign in Avignon.
From Amboise and Nime he will come the length of Indre,
He will be scratched at Poitiers and his wings ruined at Saintes,
Before Boni....(incomplete line)

Blois is a city in northern Central France; it was the residence of the counts of Blois, and became a favorite residence of French kings.

However, since "Blois" in Celtic means wolves, most likely Nostradamus mentioned it as an indication of the Arab Anti-Christ who will act wolfishly. **Avignon** is a city in southeast France.

Amboise is a town in northwest Central France, in Indre-et-Loire department (county). **Nime** (or older Nismes) is a manufacturing and commercial city in south France, 64 miles northwest of Marseille. **Indre** is a functional department of central France. Also a river, 165 miles long, in central France, flows into the Loire river.

Poitiers is a city in west central France. In 732 A.D., the Arabs were defeated at Poitiers and Tours and were forced to retreat to Spain. **Saintes** is an industrial city in west France.

Line four in this quatrain has been tampered with. **Boni** is most likely Bonifacio, a fortress-like town in the south point of Corsica, France. It is situated on a narrow peninsula with steep cliffs on three sides, on the Strait of Bonifacio. Apparently the Arab Anti-Christ will install his military headquarters there, taking advantage of its strategic position.

GENEVA UNDER SIEGE

9:44 "Migrez, migrez de Geneve trestout/Saturne d'or en fer se changera/Le contre RAYPOZ exterminera tous/Avant l'advant le ciel signes fera."

Everybody, migrate, migrate from Geneva,
Saturn from gold to iron will change.
RAYPOZ will exterminate all who oppose him.
Before the onslaught the sky will show signs.

Geneva is the capital of Geneva canton in southwest Switzerland, at the south tip of Lake Geneva on the Rhone river.

The **golden Saturn** represents peace and the springtime of humanity. **Iron** is a metaphor for swords and war, hence the changing of Saturn to iron signifies the coming of war, doom, misfortune, and darkness.

RAYPOZ is an anagram for "Apo Rayz." **Rayz** in Arabic means a leader or a chieftain. It's just a title, similar to "El Cid" which was given to the Spanish hero Rodrigo Dias de Vivar by the Moors. "Apo" is a proposition.

"Apo or Abu Rayz" can roughly be translated to: The father of all the leaders. The one who will exterminate all who oppose him is the Arab Anti-Christ.

The **signs** in the sky in line four could be missiles and air power or it could refer to supernatural happenings in the sky.

HUNGER AND THIRST IN GENEVA

2:64 "Sécher de faim, de soif gent Geneuoise/Espoir prochain viendra au défaillir/Sur point tremblant sera loi Gebenoise/Classe au grand port ne se peut accueillir."

The people of Geneva are weakened from hunger and thirst.
Hope in sight will steadily fail them.
The law of Cevennes will be on the point of trembling,
The fleet cannot be received at the great port.

Cevennes or ancient Cebenna is an old district in France, comprising the region of the Cevennes Mts. in south France. In the Middle Ages it was a refuge for Protestants. Hence the law of Ceveness in line three refers to protestant nations, like England. The **great port** in line four could be London.

THE INHABITANTS OF GENEVA ARE DESTROYED

10:92 "Devant le père l'enfant sera tué/Le père après entre cordes de jonc/Geneuois people sera esvertue/Gisant le chef au milieu comme un tronc."

The child will be killed in front of his dad,
Afterward the father will be seized.
The people of Geneva will be destroyed,
The leader lying [dead] in the middle like a trunk.

The **child** and the **father** are metaphors, respectively for the Swiss people/army and the country of Switzerland.

Esvertue in the French verse is derived from Latin "everto" which means: I destroy, ruin, overthrow.

The **trunk** in line four is originally from the Latin word "truncus," which means a mutilated body, a headless trunk.

MOTHER SHIPTON'S PROPHECIES

The prophecies of Mother Shipton (1488–1561) speak about a comet, "a fiery dragon and the dragon's tail," causing havoc to earth at the end of twentieth century or the beginning of the new one. She also tells about extraterrestrials coming to earth in "silver serpents" (UFOs) to usher in the earth's Golden Age.

(More of Mother Shipton's prophecies has been published in the *Nexus* magazine)

In nineteen hundred and twenty six
Build houses light of straw and sticks.
For then shall mighty wars be planned
And fire and sword shall sweep the
   land.

When pictures seem alive with
   movements free
When boats like fish swim beneath the
   sea
When men like birds shall scour the sky
Then half the world, deep drenched in
   blood shall die.

For those who live the century through
In fear and trembling this shall do.
Flee to the mountains and the dens
To bog and forest and wild fens.

For storms will rage and oceans roar
When Gabriel stands on sea and shore
And as he blows his wondrous horn
Old worlds die and new be born.

A fiery Dragon will cross the sky
Six times before this Earth shall die
Mankind will tremble and frightened be
For the sixth heralds in this prophecy.

For seven days and seven nights
Man will watch this awesome sight.
The tides will rise beyond their ken
To bite away the shores, and then
The mountains will begin to roar
And earthquakes split the plain to
   shore.

And flooding waters, rushing in
Will flood the lands with such a din
That mankind cowers in muddy fen
And snarls about his fellow men.

Not every soul on Earth will die
As the Dragon's tail goes sweeping by
Not every land on Earth will sink
But these will wallow in stench and
   stink
Of rotting bodies of beast and man
Of vegetation crisped on land.

But the land that rises from the sea
Will be dry and clean and soft and free
Of mankind's dirt and therefore be
The source of man's new dynasty.
And those that live will ever fear
The Dragon's tail for many year
 But time erases memory
You think it strange. But it will be.

And before the race is built anew
A silver serpent comes to view
And spew out men of like unknown
To mingle with the Earth now grown
Cold from its heat, and these men can
Enlighten the minds of future man
To intermingle and show them how
To live and love and thus endow
The children with the second sight.
A natural thing so that they might
Grow graceful, humble, and when they
   do
The Golden Age will stand anew.

The Dragon's tail is but a sign
For mankind's fall and man's decline.
And before this prophecy is done
I shall be burned at the stake, at one
My body singed and my soul set free
You think I utter blasphemy
You're wrong. These things have come
   to me
This prophecy will come to be.

The Catholic monarchs, Ferdinard of Aragon
and Isabella of Castile. They are buried in the
Renaissance cathedral in Granada.

Chapter 7

THE WAR IN SPAIN

• • • • • • • • • • • • • • • •

Spain was conquered by Moslems from North Africa during 711-719. Most of Spain was ruled by Ommiad dynasty of Cordoba during 756-1031, except in north where there arose various small Christian states. Moorish Spain was ruled by Almoravides after 1090 and by Almohades after 1147. It was gradually reconquered by Christian states of Castile and Aragon. Christian Spain united in 1479 as result of marriage (1469) of Ferdinand II of Aragon and Isabella of Castile and conquered Granada, last kindgom of Moors, in 1492.

Some quatrains of Nostradamus indicate a new Moslem invasion into southern Spain during the coming World War III.

THE ARAB ANTI-CHRIST TO VEX SPAIN

5:55 "De la felice Arabie contrade/Naîtra puissant de la loi Mahometique/Vexer l'Espagne, conquester la Grenade/Et plus par mer à la gent Ligustique."

Of the pleasant land of Arabia,
The strong one of the Muhammadan law will be born.
He will vex Spain and conquer Granada
And the Ligurian people also from the sea.

The **pleasant land** is the promised land (Palestine or modern Israel) according to the Holy Scriptures - Daniel 8:9, Zechariah 7:14, Psalm 106:24, Jeremiah 3:19.
(However, in the Wall-Map of Europe (IMAGO MUNDI), Amsterdam 1595, the southern region of modern Saudi Arabia is indicated as "Arabia Felix.")
The **strong one** who is born into the religion of Islam is the Arab Anti-Christ.
Granada is a province in southern Spain. Its capital Granada was founded by the Moors (a mixed North African people of Berber and Arabic stock) in the eighth century. In 1492 it was captured by the Spaniards ending Moorish power in Spain.

The **Ligurians** are of pre-Indo-European stock who lived in southwest Europe. Presently, Liguria is an autonomous region in northwest Italy, on the Ligurian Sea between France and Tuscany. Its capital is the seaport Genoa. In this quatrain, Nostradamus mentioned the Ligurian people as an indication for all Italy.

SPAIN TAKEN CAPTIVE

5:14 "Saturne et Mars en Leo Espaigne captive/Par chef Lybique au conflict attrapé/Proche de Malte, Heredde prince vive/Et Romain sceptre sera par Coq frappé."

Saturn and Mars in Leo; Spain is captive;
Entrapped in the conflict by the African leader.
Near Malta, the Heir is taken alive;
And the Roman scepter will be struck down by the Cock.

In the first line, Nostradamus is making a reference to an astrological conjunction of Saturn and Mars in Leo. Also Saturn in Leo indicates a downfall; and when Mars is in Leo, its fiery warlike feature is accentuated.

The Republic of **Malta** is an independent state, consisting of three islands in the Mediterranean Sea, about 58 miles south of Sicily, Italy. The major island is Malta; the smaller islands are Comino and Gozo.

The **Roman scepter** in line four refers to the sovereignty of modern Italy. The **Cock** is the Arab Anti-Christ.

AT GRANADA, THE CROSS IS PUSHED BACK
BY THE MOSLEMS

3:20 "Par les contrées du grand fleuve Bethique/Loin d'Ibere au Royaume de Grenade/Croix repoussées par gens Mahometique/Un de Cordube trahira la contrade."

In the regions of the great river Guadalquiver;
Far from Ebro, at the kingdom of Granada,
The Cross is pushed back by the Moslems.
Someone from Cordoba will betray his homeland.

Guadalquiver is a river in Andalusia, south Spain, it flows west and southwest into Gulf of Cadiz; 408 miles long. **Ebro** is a river in northeast Spain, 565 miles long. The ancient **kingdom of Granada** in Upper Andalusia, was divided in 1833 into the modern provinces of Granada, Almeria, and Malaga. The city of Granada is located in Sierra Nevada Mts., 80 miles southeast of Cordoba, the capital of the Cordoba province in Andalusia.

The **Cross** in line three refers to Christianity. Apparently the Spanish Army will be defeated in southern Spain, and the Moslems will recapture Andalusia. However, in his Epistle to King Henry, Nostradamus mentions the eventual defeat of the Moslems once more. He wrote: "And a new incursion will be made by the maritime shores, wishing to deliver the Sierra Morena [located in south Spain] from the first Moslem recapture. Their assault will not at all be in vain."

THE CRESCENT LOWERED AGAIN IN SPAIN

10:95 "Dans les Espaignes viendra Roi très-puissan/Par mer et terre subjuguant le Midi/Ce mal fera, rebaissant le croissant/Baisser les ailes à ceux du Vendredi."

**A very strong king will rise to power in Spain,
Subjugating the South by land and sea.
He will Injure and lower again the crescent,
Clipping the wings of those of Friday.**

The **crescent** and **those of friday** both are allusions to the Moslems.

The **South** is Andalusian region of southern Spain, of some 33,695 sq. miles. It is divided into Upper Andalusia (the valley of upper Guadalquiver), and lower Andalusia (the valley of lower Guadalquiver).

In 711–1492, Andalusia was subjugated by the Moors. Lower Andalusia was reconquered by Christians in 1212; Upper Andalusia, or the Moorish kingdom of Granada, was reconquered by Ferdinand and Isabella in 1492.

In Medieval Chronicles, Egypt was referred to as Babylon.

From Babylon [=modern Egypt],
The daughter of the persecuted [=the modern state of Israel],
Miserable and sad,
Her wings will be cut.
(8:96, page 104)

"O Jerusalem, Jerusalem, who kills the prophets and stones those who are sent to her! How often I wanted to gather your children together, the way a hen gathers her chicks under her wings, and you were unwilling." (Matthew 23:37).

"I could see Israel becoming isolated from the rest of the world. As things worsened, there were images of Israel preparing for war against other countries, including Russia and a Chinese-and-Arab consortium. Jerusalem was some-how at the eye of this conflict, but I am not sure exactly how. Some incident in that holy city had served to trigger this war. [Most likely the rebuilding of the Jewish temple]."

Dannion Brinkley

CHAPTER 8

THE WAR IN THE LAND OF PROMISE

• • • • • • • • • • • • • • • • •

THE HOLOCAUST

9:53 "Le Neron jeune dans les trois cheminess/Fera de pages vifs pour ardoir jeter/Heureux qui loin sera de tels menees/Trois de son sang le feront mort guetter."

The Nero in the furnaces the three young
Boys will hurl live in order to burn them.
Not approving of such undertakings,
Three of his kind will plot to kill him.

In this verse, Nostradamus referred to Hitler by the name of Nero, the Roman emperor known for his cruelty, instability, and the persecution of the Christians.

In Chapter 3 of the book of Daniel, there is the story of three Hebrew youths: Hananiah, Mishael and Azariah, captives of Nebuchadnezzar, King of Babylon, who cast them into a furnace of blazing fire for refusing to worship him. Hence, Nostradamus' use of a simile, indicating the Jewish Holocaust by the Nazis during World War II.

The three chief German personalities who did not approve Hitler's acts and attempted to assassinate him were Karl Goerdeler, General Beck and Colonel Von Stauffen Berg who placed the bomb that slightly injured Hitler.

THE OCCUPATION OF A NEW LAND

3:97 "Nouvelle loi terre neuve occuper/Vers la Syrie, Iudée et Palestine/Le grand empire barbare corruer/Avant que Phebés son siècle determine."

New law to occupy new land
Toward Syria, Judea and Palestine.

The great barbarian empire to fall down,
Before the Moon finishes its cycle.

The first two lines refer to the birth of the modern state of Israel after World War II.

The **great barbarian empire** is the short-lived Nazi empire of Hitler. The **Phebes** in the French verse is from the Latin Phoebe, the Moon. The period of the moon's revolution is twenty-eight-and-a-half days which the ancients divided into three phases - waxing, full, and waning; or infancy, maturity, and decay.

The fall of the Nazi empire before the Moon finishes its cycle or phase indicates the death of the empire in its early stages. History proved Nostradamus to be right.

FROM BABYLON HER WINGS WILL BE CUT

8:96 "La synagogue stérile sans nul fruit/Sera reçue entre les infi-deles/De Babylon la fille du poursuit/Misère et triste lui tranchera les ailes."

The sterile synagogue without any fruit,
Will be received among the infidels.
From Babylon, the daughter of the persecuted,
Miserable and sad, her wings will be cut.

The first two lines refer to the settlement of the uprooted and homeless Jews in the land of Palestine, among the Moslems (**the infidels**).

Babylon in this quatrain is Egypt. In Nostradamus' time, Cairo, the capital of Egypt, was referred to as "Babylon." In the Wall-Map of Europe (IMAGO MUNDI), printed in Amsterdam, 1595, "Cairo" is clearly associated with the word Babylon.

The **miserable daughter of the persecuted** whose wings are going to be clipped is the modern state of Israel and her Jewish inhabitants.

THE PROFANATION OF THE TEMPLE

3:45 "Les cinq étranges entrés dans le temple/Leur sang viendra la terre profaner/Aux Tholosains sera bien dur example/D'un qui viendra ses lois exterminer."

Five strangers having entered the temple,
Their blood will profane the ground.
To the "Toulousans" a hard example will be made
By one who will come to exterminate their laws.

The **five strangers** refer to five Moslem activists who will desecrate the rebuilt Jewish temple by killing themselves and shedding their blood inside the new temple.

The **Toulousans** or the people of Toulouse in line three refer to the Jewish people in Israel who at last are able to rebuild the Third Temple on holy Moslem ground. In the Middle Ages, the city of Toulouse in France was a center for radical "heretics" who rebelled against the Vatican, hence the metaphoric use of their name by Nostradamus.

Presently there is speculation in Israel that the Ark of the Covenant has been recovered and is safely awaiting the day when the Jews rebuild their prized Third Temple.

The one who will make a hard example of the Jews and exterminate their laws is the coming Arab Anti-Christ.

THE FURNACES ARE REBUILT

9:17 "Le tiers premier pis que ne fit Neron/Videz vaillant que sang human répandre/R'edifier fera le forneron/Siècle d'or mort, nouveau Roi grand escalandre."

The Third does worse than the first Nero,
Lacking gallantry, [will cause] human blood to flow copiously.
He will rebuild the furnaces.
A golden period is dead, the new King [will make] a great scene.

The **Third** is the Arab Anti-Christ. The **first Nero** is the infamous Roman emperor, born Lucius Domitius Ahenobarbus. He persecuted, massacred and tortured the Christians in a cruel way. The Third Anti-Christ from the Middle East will emulate Nero, surpassing him in cruelty and insanity.

The **Furnaces** in line three is a reference to the Jewish Holocaust by the Nazis.

The **golden cycle** or period refers to a time of peace. And the **new King** is the coming Arab Anti-Christ.

The prophets Daniel and Hosea did also prophesy the destruction of the state of Israel and the Third Temple. Daniel stated: "Then after the sixty-two weeks the Messiah will be cut off and have nothing, and the people of the prince who is to come [i.e. the Arab Anti-Christ] will destroy the city and the sanctuary" (Daniel 9:26). While Hosea declared: For behold, they will go because of destruction; Egypt will gather them up, Memphis will bury them. Weeds will take over their treasures of silver [of the rebuilt temple]; thorns will be in their tents (Hosea 9:6).

Also the words of Jesus Christ in the gospel of Luke bear witness to the same end-time event. Luke 21:20–27 states: "But when you see Jerusalem surrounded by armies, then recognize that her desolation is at hand. Then let those who are in Judea flee to the mountains, and let those who are in the midst of the city depart, and let not those who are in the country enter the city; because these are days of vengeance, in order that all things which are written may be fulfilled. Woe to those who are with child and to those who nurse babies in those days; for there will be great distress upon the land, and wrath to this people, and they will fail by the edge of the sword, and will be led captive into all the nations; and Jerusalem will be trampled under foot by the Gentiles until the times of the Gentiles be fulfilled.

"And there will be signs in sun and moon and stars, and upon the earth dismay among nations, in perplexity at the roaring of the sea and the waves, men fainting from fear and the expectation of the things which are coming upon the world; for the power of the heavens will be shaken, and then they will see the Son of Man COMING IN A CLOUD with power and great glory."

In his *Epistle to the King* Nostradamus confirmed the same, he wrote: "And the place which was once the habitation of Abraham [Israel/Palestine] will be assaulted by persons who hold the Thursdays in veneration. And this city of Achan [=Jerusalem] will be surrounded and assailed on all sides by a most powerful of armed people....The sepulcher, for a long time an object of such great veneration, will remain in the open, exposed to the sight of the heaven, the sun and the moon. And the holy place will be converted into a stable for a herd large and small, and used for profane purposes."

"For just as the lightning comes from the east, and flashes even to the west, so shall the coming of the Son of Man be."

The Book of Matthew 24:27

And another angel, a second one, followed, saying, "Fallen, fallen is Babylon the great, she who made all nations drink of the wine of the passion of her immorality." Revelation 14:8

"Ogmios Will approach the great Byzantium;/ the Barbarian League will be expelled./ Of the two laws, the heathen one will fail." Century 5, Quatrain 80.

Chapter 9

THE FALL OF THE GREAT BABYLON

• • • • • • • • • • • • • • • •

THOSE OF THE ARCTIC POLE ARE UNITED

6:21 "Quand ceux du pôle arctique unis ensemble/En Orient grand effrayeur et crainte/Élu nouveau soutenu le grand tremble/Rodes, Bisance de sang barbare teinte."

When those of the arctic pole are united together,
In the Orient [there will be] great fear and dread.
A newly appointed one will sustain a great deal of damage;
Rhodes, Byzantium are tainted with Barbarian blood.

Those of the arctic pole are the USA, Canada, Russia and north Europe, all united against the Moselm empire of the Arab Anti-Christ; a new alliance that will send shivers through his empire; the Anti-Christ himself, sensing his approaching end, will panic and become frightened.

A newly appointed one in line three refers to a military appointment by Anti-Christ, and the **Barbarian blood** is the blood of his defeated army in modern Greece (**Rhodes**) and Turkey (**Byzantium**).

THE KING OF EUROPE WILL COME AGAINST THE KING OF BABYLON

10:86 "Comme un griffon viendra le Roi d'Europe/Accompangné de ceux d'Aquilon/De rouges et blancs conduira grande troupe/Et iront contre le Roi de Babylon."

The King of Europe will come like a griffin,
Accompanied by those of the North.
He will lead a great army of reds and whites,
And they will go against the King of Babylon.

The **King of Europe** in this quatrain refers to "Ogmios," the French hero who will lead the campaign against the Arab Anti-Christ. **Those of the North** are the USA, Canada, Russia and northern European countries.

Griffin is a mythical animal with the body and hind legs of a lion, and the head, wings, and claws of an eagle.

The **King of Babylon** is the Arab Anti-Christ from Egypt, Babylon (i.e. Egypt) being a reference to his empire.

At the beginning of the conflict, Russia, Iran and the Arabs will be allies in their conquest of the West. This quatrain implies that later on Russia will change sides.

Presently (1994), there is a concern in the West about Russian neo-imperialist aspirations, which are spearheaded by Mr. Zhirinovsky and his nationalist party. Zhirinovsky and the Russian military are known friends of the Arabs.

THE FALL OF THE HEATHEN LAW

5:80 "Logmion grande Bisance approchera/Chassée sera la Barbarique Ligue/Des deux lois l'une l'estinique lâchera/Barbare et franche en perpétuelle brique."

Ogmios will approach the great Byzantium,
The Barbarian League will be driven away.
Of the two laws, the heathen one will fail,
The Barbarian and the true [laws] in perpetual strife.

Ogmios (the Celtic equivalent of Hercules in mythological lore) is the French hero who will defeat the Anti-Christ and his Barbaric League.

The heathen or barbaric law refers to the Moslem religion as expounded by the Anti-Christ, the true law being that of Christianity.

THE GREAT CITY IS MADE DESOLATE

3:84 "La grande cité sera bien désolée/Des habitants un seul n'y demeurera/Mur, sexe, temple, et vierge violée/Par fer, feu, peste, canon peuple mourra."

The great city will be desolate for good,
Of the inhabitants none will remain there.
Wall, sex, temple and virgin are violated.
By iron, fire, pestilence, and cannon her people will die.

The **great city** is the empire of the Arab Anti-Christ. There is also a mention of it in the book of Revelation (chapter 17, verse 18): "And the woman whom you saw is the great city, which reigns over the kings of the earth." The "woman" whom St. John saw in his vision was the one upon whose forehead was written the name: BABYLON THE GREAT, THE MOTHER OF HARLOTS AND OF THE ABOMINATIONS OF THE EARTH (Revelation 17:4, 5). God called the empire of the Anti-Christ: Babylon the Great.

The prophets Isaiah and Jeremiah also have prophesied about Babylon the Great: "And Babylon, the beauty of kingdoms, the glory of the Chaldeans' pride, will be as when God overthrew Sodom and Gomorra. It will never be inhabited or lived in from generation to generation; nor will the Arab pitch his tent there, nor will shepherds make their flocks lie down there. But desert creatures will lie down there, and their houses will be full of owls, ostriches also will live there, and shaggy goats will frolic there. And hyenas will howl in their fortified towers and jackals in their luxurious palaces. Her fateful time also will soon come and her days will not be prolonged (Isaiah 13:19-22)."

"So the land quakes and writhes, for the purposes of the Lord against Babylon stand, to make the land of Babylon a desolation without inhabitants. The mighty men of Bablyon have ceased fighting, they stay in the strongholds; their strength is exhausted, they are becoming like women; their dwelling places are set on fire, the bars of her gates are broken. One courier runs to meet another, and one messenger to meet another, to tell the king of Babylon that his city has been captured from end to end; the fords also have been seized, and they have burned the marshes with fire and the men of war are terrified (Jeremiah 51:29-32)."

"Her cities have become an object of horror, a parched land and a desert, a land in which no man lives, and through which no son of man passes. And I shall punish Bel in Babylon, and I shall make what he has swallowed come out of his mouth; and the nations will no longer stream to him. Even the wall of Babylon has fallen down!" (Jeremiah 51:43, 44).

AMERICA

"This is the exulted city which dwells securely, who says in her heart, 'I am, and there is no one besides me.' how she has become a desolation, a resting place for beasts! Everyone who passes by her will hiss and wave his hand in contempt"
(the Book of Zephaniah 2:15)

Appendix

ABOUT THE UNITED STATES

•   •   •   •   •   •   •   •   •   •   •   •   •   •   •   •   •   •   •

In his epistle to the King, Nostradamus writes that most of his prophecies "have been integrated with astronomical calculations corresponding to the years, months and weeks of the regions, countries and most of the town and cities of all Europe, including Africa and part of Asia, where most of all these coming events are to transpire" thus leaving an obvious gap concerning the fate of the USA, the sole super power on earth in our present decade.

In order to somehow fill that gap, several contemporary prophecies have been appended to this work.

THE MAN OF GOD FROM ROMANIA

For 25 years, Dumitru Duduman was a faithful pastor and bible smuggler in his native land - Romania. In 1980, after delivering over 100,000 New Testaments, which were given away at the Moscow Olympic, Dumitru was arrested in August of the same year. He was beaten in a Romanian jail almost daily and even tortured in an electric chair.

His days of persecution and torture came to an end when in 1984, Dumitru and his family were exiled to the United States where he founded a charitable ministry to help the poor Christians and orphans in Romania, now that the dictatorship was over there.

Dumitru tells his true story and gives more prophetic messages in his autobiographical book "Through the Fire Without Burning." His ministry also publishes a monthly newsletter. The address of his ministry is: HAND OF HELP, Box 3494, Fullerton, California 92634, USA. The phone: (714) 447-1313.

MESSAGES FROM GOD

As soon as Dumitru and his family were settled in California in 1984, the angel of the Lord told Dumitru - among other things - that the day will come when the angel will punish the citizens of Los Angeles, Las Vegas, New York and other cities because of their sin. Their sin having reached into heaven, God will punish them just as he punished Sodom and Gomorrah.

The angel added that when the Americans will believe that all is peaceful and safe, the Russians, discovering the whereabouts of U.S. missile and nuclear warhead storage sites and factories, will launch a first nuclear attack on those facilities and cause the USA to burn.

A short time after, the angel gives more details: "When the Americans think that there is peace and they are safe, from the middle of the nation some people will rise against the government who will become busy with internal problems. Then from the ocean, from Cuba, Nicaragua, Mexico (and from two more nations) they will bomb the nuclear warehouses. When they explode, America will burn....but when America burns, the Lord will raise China, Japan and other nations to go against the Russians. They will defeat the Russians and push them all the way to the gates of Paris, France. Over there they will make a [peace] treaty and appoint the Russians as their leader. They then will unite against Israel."

In 1991, Dumitru wrote: "So many people were asking, 'When will it happen? When will America burn?' I prayed and asked God, 'What will I tell people when they ask me when it will happen?' That night an angel came and touched me on the hand and said, 'Dumitru, wake up! Sit up! Get your Bible and read **Hosea 4:6-9** and **Hosea 6:1-3**...Tell the people of America that one day with the Lord is a thousand years, and a thousand years as one day. If they will repent and turn back to God, they will make it through the second day [The second millennium A.D.?] to the third day [the third millennium A.D.?]. If they don't they will not make it.' "

The present resurgence of nationalism in Russia, and the revival of the Russian dream of a Slavic brotherhood stretching all the way to the Balkans are bringing the world closer to a global warfare and giving validity to the prophecies of "The Man of God From Romania."

THE SEER OF BAYSIDE

Veronica Lueken, the seer of Bayside, is a wife and mother of five children. She is seventy years old and lives on Long Island, New York. (Veronica passed away on Aug. 3, 1995.)

The story of her heavenly visitations goes back to the year 1968 when St. Theresa appeared to her and began giving her poems and sacred writings by dictation.

Since 1970, Veronica has been receiving visitations from Mother Mary and has been instructed to disseminate the messages given to her throughout the whole world.

The address of her ministry is: Our Lady of the Roses, Mary Help of Mothers Shrine, P O Box 52, Bayside, New York 11361, USA. Phone: (718) 961-8865.

MESSAGES FROM MOTHER MARY AND JESUS

In late 1990, Virgin Mary appeared to Veronica in her bedroom and gave her the following message about a great war erupting suddenly. Apparently Our Lady was speaking about the coming World War III: "Dear child, you will write just as you receive it from Me. You will be unable to go to the holy grounds this evening; hence you will disseminate this message to the world as soon as possible. I, your Mother, and protectress of the world's children, do beg you now to repent of your sins against the teachings of the Eternal Father - sins of the flesh and the intellect. A great war will erupt suddenly, such as has not been seen from the beginning of creation. Countries shall disappear in moments from the face of the earth. Will you not listen to Me before it is too late? You do not have much time left. I come to you as a Protectress of peace. Unless you repent of your abortions, the murders of the unborn, and return to lives of prayer and contemplation of the mysteries of the Eternal Father, given by writings - the Bible, the book of life and love - I cannot save you from the conflagration that lies ahead. Seek God in prayer, penance, and atonement. My tears fall upon all mankind. Will you not solace Me, My children?"

In other messages to Veronica, Mother Mary has said that revolutions will happen in Africa and Europe. The revolution in Italy will force the pope to flee Rome. Then a great cataclysmic warning will be given to mankind; if it is not heeded, then mankind will receive the worldwide Great Chastisement, namely World War III, followed by a surprise entry of a fiery comet into the earth's atmosphere. In total, three-quarters of all mankind will be destroyed.

In June 2, 1979, the Lord Jesus spoke through Veronica saying: "I have often warned you that unless you turn back from your present road - a road that means the destruction of souls and the eventual physical destruction of many nations upon your earth - unless you turn back now, what more can I say, but to acknowledge that from the Eternal Father a great warning - preceded by a minor warning upon earth -

shall be set upon mankind. After this, unless you turn back and do great penance, make atonement to the Eternal Father for your offences to Him, you will receive a great chastisement."

In March 26, 1983, Jesus, in a vision, touched on the same subject, saying: "As My Mother has told you before, I will repeat again. There will be minor chastisement,   and then will come the great warning and the greatest of chastisements, one such as has never been seen before in your nation or the nations of the world and we pray will never be seen again." On June 18, 1986, Jesus repeated again: "For soon there will come upon you the great Chastisement. It comes in two parts, My child and my children: the Third World War, and also the Ball of Redemption."

However, this world will not end yet. On December 24, 1974, Mother Mary said: "The world as you know it shall be changed, not completely annihilated as in the time of Noah, but changed." And on November 25, 1978, Jesus said: "You are in the end days. It will not be the end of the earth or the world, but it will be the end of your era, the end of time as you know it."

THE MAN WITH VISIONS OF CATACLYSMIC EARTH CHANGES

Mr. Scallion used to be a communication consultant, with a scientific/electronic background. While in a hospital bed for observation because of a sudden health crisis, a supernatural female being of light paid a visit to him in a vision and gave him prophetic instructions. The next morning he felt fine, but to his surprise he found himself a changed man with gifts of prophecy and paranormal strange powers and abilities.

He could see and read auras, and allegedly could look inside bodies and detect diseases. However, mostly, he began receiving visions and information about geological events, specially cataclysmic disasters, simultaneous tornados, earthquakes, hurricanes and volcanic eruptions; all exploding across our planet in the years leading up to the millennium. Some of the changes occur abruptly, others give warning signs.

He prophetically speaks of the period from 1998 to 2001, as a time of great geological events and changes, "of the earth becoming very quiet the animals are quiet, then a wind picks up from the east, with hurricane velocity. Then the sun reverses its direction in the sky, the oceans themselves bolting and land masses thrusting up."

Mr. Scallion has created a map of the future of the United States; a map that is the consolidation of the visions he has received and it represents what the United States would look-like between the years 1998 and 2001. In the new map, California is a series of islands. The Mississippi is expanded and the Great Lakes are merged. Good portions of New Jersey, New York, and New England are under water.

However, in his 1994 edition of The Future Map of the United States, Mr. Scallion mentions that "the areas of change presented in The Future Map of the United States: 1998-2001 should not be taken as absolute. They are one person's vision of what may be. In the end, Mother Nature and the way we live our lives will have the final say. I am often asked, 'Can we change these events?' If enough of us return to a life of balance and harmony, all things are possible. I believe visions and prophecy are given to enable us to change probable realities, or, at the very least, assist us in preparing for what is to come."

Mr. Scallion's prophecies are published monthly in The Earth Changes Report, the Matrix Tele-communications Network, and through Matrix Institute's audio and video programs. Phone: (603) 399-4916. The address: Matrix Institute, Inc., P. O. Box 87, Westmoreland, N.H. 03467, USA.

There are also other groups that predict earth changes, and one such group has presented the **I Am America** map purportedly showing the future North American continent after great earthquakes have occurred, with America having approximately one-half the land mass it does today.

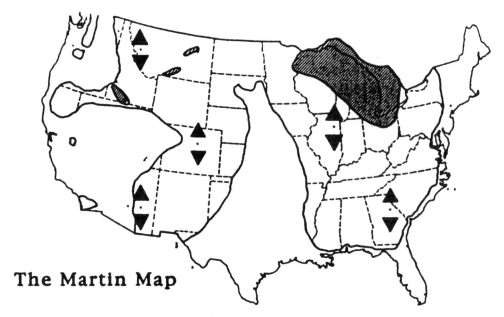

The Martin Map

The Martin Map is an update to the I Am America Map. It appeared in March 1993.

THE AUTHOR

The author of this book is mostly self-taught, and has spent half of his middle-aged life in the Mediterranean region, speaking various languages of that region.

After experiencing a spiritual regeneration in 1977, he decided to write a prophetic book. The result is this collection.

He classifies himself as an open-minded Christian, a student of the Holy Bible and a reseacher of prophecies.

THE '93 BIG BANG AT THE WORLD TRADE CENTER: A WARNING FROM GOD

On Friday, February 26, 1993, shortly after noon, a huge explosion rocked the World Trade Center in Manhattan, New York. The bomb explosion rocked the ground with the force of an earthquake. It ripped through three levels of concrete floor in the parking garage, leaving a giant open crater. The blast was felt throughout the Wall Street area and a mile away on Ellis and Liberty islands in the New York harbor.

Instantly New York City's largest building complex - visited by more than 200,000 people daily - was plunged into a maelstorm of smoke, darkness and fearful chaos. Hundreds of people were trapped in smoke-filled stairways and elevators. The area looked like a war zone - total devastation. All of lower Manhattan was held in the grippe of traffic snarls and anxiety. 50,00 people were evacuated from the 110-story twin Towers; 1042 were injured mostly by smoke inhalation or minor burns, but dozens had cuts, bruises, broken bones or serious burns. 450 of the injured were treated at hospitals. Six were dead.

As a result of the blast, all the commodities exchanges closed for the day. The Commodity Exchange Inc. (the Comex) closed trading about 1:30 p.m. on various metal contracts, including gold, silver, and copper. In the New York Mercantile exchange, the world's leading petroleum market, trading paused in the exchange's oil and precious metals pits. The disruption on Wall Street slowed the level of trading in the stock and bond markets, and many large brokerage firms and banks in lower Manhattan let some employees go home early. Four hours after the explosion a bomb threat forced the evacuation of the Empire State Building.

The unprecedented incident sent a shock wave across the USA and around the world, and caused the closing of the two Towers of the World Trade Center - which alone did business in 300 million dollars weekly - for an unspecified period of time.

God, through the prophet Zephania, did prophesy about that shocking event. Verses 10-11 from chapter one of the book of Zephania declare:

And on that day, declares the Lord, there will be the sound of a cry from the Fish Gate, a wail from the Second Quarter, and a loud crash from the hills.

Wail, O inhabitants of the Mortar, for all the people of Canaan will be silenced; all who weigh out silver will be cut off.

In this prophecy the **Fish Gate** refers to the N.Y. harbor; the **Second Quarter** to the second Tower of the World Trade Center which sustained more damage than the first one; the **hills** refers to the basement layers beneath the Towers; the **Mortar** to New York City. The **people of Canaan** are known to live in coastal cities and engage in banking, commerce, and trade.

In the same chapter of the book of Zephania (1:14-16), the prophecy goes on:

Near is the great day of the Lord,
Near and coming very quickly;
Listen, the day of the Lord!
In it the warrior cries out bitterly.
A day of wrath is that day,
A day of trouble and distress,

A day of destruction and desolation,
A day of darkness and gloom.
A day of clouds and thick darkness,
A day of trumpet and battle cry,
Against the fortified cities
And the high corner towers.

Prophecies of doom are given by a loving God so that they would fail. It is human impassivity that makes them come true.

In recent years dozens of paramilitary Patriot groups have sprung up in an estimated 34 states. All have an implacable opposition to gun control and they believe that the government will do anything to restrict their freedoms guaranteed in the Constitution and the Bill of Rights. Many share opposition to taxes, and many harbor theories that the government wants to control the lives of Americans. The call to take up arms against the government have also been embraced by other grass-roots movements on the American right.

A wave of violence, intimidation and threats against anyone associated with the government has been building in a half-dozen states. In Montana, Idaho, Washington and elsewhere, government employees at all levels are cast as members of a "New World Order" working to take over the United States.

The tragic Oklahoma City bombing, on 19 April 1995, has brought the anti-government movement into the limelight. The publicity has helped increase the number of citizen militias by making people aware of their movement. Unfortunately, the militias are fostering vicious anti-government thinking that if followed to its logical end will lead in one direction: Armed civil conflict.

In 1984, a prophecy was given (see page 114) stating that before Russia lunches a nuclear first strike on USA "from the middle of the nation some people will rise against the government who will become busy with internal problems." Are we going to see that prophecy being fulfilled in the coming years?

SPACE PEOPLE ARE REAL

"This Awareness indicates that the basis reality is that there are and were space people, persons who travel interdimensionally and through space, who move in and out of this dimension, or on and off this planet, from the surface and into the inner parts.

"That the alleged angels with the wings which are often spoken of or depicted in ancient myths, are in fact representatives from certain other frequencies and may actually appear in physical form as beings with wings. They are interdimensional beings whose genetic heredity is different and along different lines from those of the physical body. However, in many instances, these are simply symbolic in nature and are symbolic representations of entities who have the ability to fly by use of crafts or flying machines.

"That the dark forces [the Grey and Reptoid aliens] prefer that entities think that the UFOs are but a hoax, or that they do not exist, or that if entities do believe they exist, that they come from other planets, that the earth's surface is the only place wherein life exists, and that all of these concepts and stories of interdimensional beings or of angels and fallen angels are false and unreal; for if people were to suddenly grasp that the dark forces [the Greys and Reptoids] are interdimensional beings and are popping in and out of this plane and its dimension at will, and have the ability to influence entities' mind and behavior, it would destroy a great part of the deception which they weave and use in order to control and direct and entrap the masses on this plane.

"This Awareness indicates that it is the dark forces who seek to prevent entities from discovering the true nature and origins of the flying saucers and of interdimensional realities, and of life after death, and of those various mysteries which are, in spite of them and their efforts, are being revealed more and more."

Cosmic Awareness

• • •

"Yes, there are spiritual beings from etheric or invisible realms who teach and love humans, sometimes appearing in dreams and visions or in physical meetings. But there are also the physical contacts with those we term extraterrestrials and possibly other life forms less well-known to us."

Virginia Essence

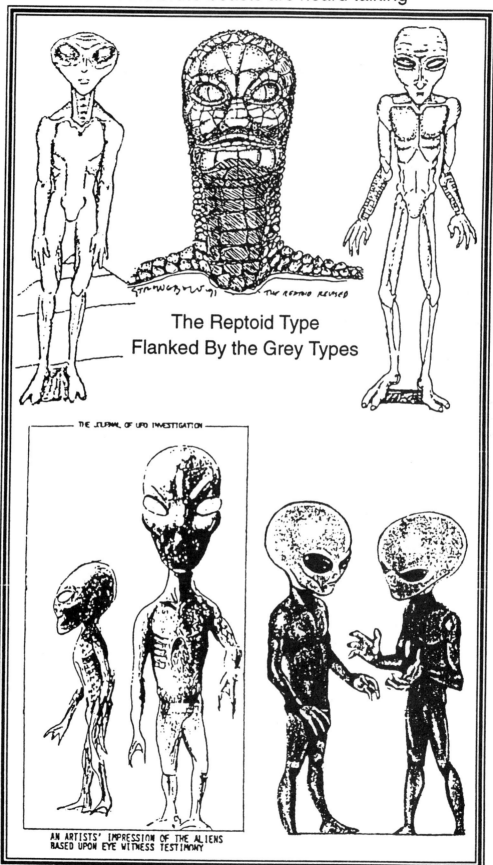

The Reptoid Type
Flanked By the Grey Types

THE JOURNAL OF UFO INVESTIGATION

AN ARTISTS' IMPRESSION OF THE ALIENS
BASED UPON EYE WITNESS TESTIMONY

Supplement 1

GALACTIC WARS

• • • • • • • • • • • • • • • •

Century 1, Quatrain 64:
De nuit soleil penseront avoir vu
Quand le pourceau demi-homme on verra,
Bruit, chant, bataille, au ciel battre apercu
Et bestes brutes a parler l'on orra.

**They will think they have seen the sun at night
When they will see the pig half-man.
Noise, song, battle, fighting in the sky perceived,
And brute beasts are heard talking.**

William Cooper claims to be a former United States Naval Intelligence Briefing Team member. His book "Behold A Pale Horse," published in 1991, exposes the alien presence on earth. In the Chapter twelve. Mr. Cooper writes that "During the years following World War II....the United States Government discovered that an alien spacecraft piloted by insect-like beings from a totally incomprehensible culture had crashed in the desert of New Mexico. Between January 1947 and December 1952 at least 16 crashed or downed alien craft, 65 alien bodies, and 1 live alien were recovered....Sightings of UFOs were so numerous that serious investigation and debunking of each report became impossible utilizing the existing intelligence assets....During these early years the United States Air Force and the CIA exercised complete control over the Alien Secret....Later the National Security Act was established to oversee the intelligence community and especially the alien endeavor....President Truman had been keeping our allies, including the Soviet Union, informed of the developing alien problem. This had been done in case the aliens turned out to be a threat to the human race. Plans were formulated to defend the Earth in case of invasion....During Eisenhower's first year in office, 1953, at least 10 alien crashed disks were recovered along with 26 dead and 4 live aliens....In 1953, astronomers discovered large objects in space which were moving toward Earth. It was first believed that they were asteroids. Later evidence proved that the objects could only be spaceships. When the objects reached the Earth they took up a very high orbit around the equator. There were several huge ships, and their actual intent was unknown. Project Sigma, and a new project, Plato, through radio communications using the computer binary language, was able to arrange a landing that resulted in face to face contact with alien beings from another planet. Project Plato was tasked with establishing diplomatic relations with this alien space race.

"In the meantime a race of human-looking aliens (the Pleiadeans) contacted the U.S. Government. This alien group (The Plaeideans) warned us against the aliens that were orbiting the Equator and offered to help us....They demanded that we dismantle and destroy our nuclear weapons (of that time) as the major condition....Nuclear disarmament was not considered to be within the best interest of the United States. The overtures were rejected. Later in 1954 the race of large nosed Gray Aliens which had been orbiting the Earth landed at Holloman Air Force Base. A basic agreement was reached. This race identified themselves as originating from a planet around a red star in the Constellation which we call Betelgeuse (Or Betelgeux, which is a reddish supergiant star, sometimes the brightest star in the constellation Orion)....President Eisenhower met with the aliens and formal treaty between the Alien Nation and the United States of American was signed.

"The Treaty stated: The aliens would not interfere in our affairs and we would not interfere in theirs. We would keep their presence on earth a secret. They would furnish us with advanced technology and would help us in our technological development. They would not make any treaty with any other nation....By 1955 it became obvious that the aliens had deceived Eisenhower and had broken the treaty. Mutilated humans were being found along with mutilated animals all across the United States....The Soviet Union was suspected of interacting with them and this proved to be true. It was learned that the aliens had been and were then manipulating masses of people through secret societies, witchcraft, magic, the occult, and religion. After several Air Force combat air engagements with alien craft it also became apparent that our weapons were no match against them....By a secret Executive Memorandum, Eisenhower commissioned a study group to examine all the facts, evidence, lies, and deception and discover the truth of the alien question....A major finding of the alien study was that the public could not be told as it was believed that this would most certainly lead to economic collapse, collapse of religious structure, and national panic which would lead into anarchy. Secrecy thus continued. An offshoot of this finding was that if the public could not be told then the Congress could not be told.

"Another major finding was the aliens were using humans and animals for a source of glandular secretions, enzymes, hormonal secretions, blood and in horrible genetic experiments. The aliens explained these actions as necessary to their survival....and since our weapons were literally useless against the aliens, (the group known as) MJ-12 decided to continue friendly diplomatic relations with them until such time as we were able to develop a technology which would enable us to challenge them on a military basis. Overtures would have to be made to the Soviet Union, and other nations, to join forces for the survival of humanity....

"MJ has presented each new president with a (false) picture of a lost alien culture seeking to renew itself, build a home on this planet, and shower us with gifts of technology. In some cases the president was told nothing. Each president in turn has bought the story, or no story at all, hook line and sinker.

"Another contingency plan is in force and is working upon you today. It is the plan to prepare the public for eventual confrontation with an alien race. The public is being bombarded with movies, radio, advertising, and TV depicting almost every aspect of the true nature of the alien presence. This includes the good and the bad. Look around and pay attention. The aliens are planning to make their presence known and the government is preparing you for it so that there will be no panic." One of the conclusions of Mr. Cooper is that "the government has been totally deceived and we are being manipulated by an alien power which will result in the total enslavement and/or destruction of the human race. We must use any and every means available to prevent this from happening." (The Intelligence Service, P.O. Box 1420, Show Low, AZ 85901, U.S.A.)

Robert O. Dean, a retired Command Sergeant Major who was assigned in 1963 to NATO's Supreme Headquarters Operations Center and given Cosmic Top Secret security clearance, has stated in an interview given to the author A.J.S. Rayl in 1993:

"The major conclusions in the NATO report (Assessment: An Evaluation of a Possible Military Threat to Allied Forces in Europe) blew me away....The first conclusion was that the planet and human race had been the subject of a detailed survey of some kind by several different extraterrestrial civiliations, four of which they had identified visually. One race looked almost indistinguishable from us. Another resembled humans in height, statue, and structure, but with a very gray, pasty skin tone. The third race is now popularly known as the grays, and the fourth was described as reptilian, with vertical pupils and lizardlike skin."

Page 54, April 1994 issue of OMNI (OMNI magazine, back issue department, P.O. Box 11260, Des Moines, IOWA 50340, U.S.A.

The current interpreter of Cosmic Awareness, Paul Shockly, defines C.A. as "the force that expressed itself through Jesus of Nazareth, the Buddha, Krishna, Mohammed, Edgar Cayce and other great avatars who served as 'Channels' for Heavenly Father who speaks again today as the world begins to enter the 'New Age' of spiritual consciousness and awareness.

"Since 1963 Cosmic Awareness has been communicating through carefully trained channels. Cosmic Awareness tells us not to believe anything, but to question, explore, doubt, and discover for yourself, through your own channel, what is the truth. Cosmic Awareness will only 'indicate' and 'suggest.' Neither C.A. Communications or any of the Interpreters is responsible for anything Cosmic Awareness states in any of the readings, nor does C A.C. or the Interpreters necessarily agree with the statements of Cosmic Awareness. The Interpreters interpret the energies as they see them in trance levels and are not personally responsible for what is said."

Cosmic Awareness indicated the existence of three elements in our Milky Way galaxy that work as units. "The Galactic Confederation which is made up from planet groups of many different constellations within the galaxy: Pleiades, Vega, Lyra, the Sirius system and others. They all work together to try to hinder the spread of Draconian influence. And the Draconian Federation, it is not a Confederation, but a Federation. The Draconians have absorbed those from Zeta Reticuli and have brought these entities into the Federation as mercenaries....and there is that which is called the Empire, controlled by Orion. The Draconians are under the control of the Orion Empire....As for the so-called Intergalactic Command or Intergalactic Confederation, this may be thought of more as a grouping or alliance of highly evolved spiritual beings of different star systems who have united in their common purpose of hindering the Orion Empire and Draconian Federation from capturing and enslaving other planets outside their own already held Federations and Empires" (R. of A., 1992-15, page 10).

"New visitations to earth, especially those from Orion and from the Pleiades occurred after World War II. The Pleiadeans attempted to warn governments about the Orion Grey aliens, but to no avail, and the Orion Greys created the first contract or peace pact or agreements with the United States government under Truman....in 1948 and the following years. The Zeta Reticuli Greys came later and firmed up their particular agreements with the U.S. government in the early 60's" (Revelations of Awareness, 1992-9, page 6).

"This Awareness indicates they are using implants and are abducting entities to use those entities to interface with the human population.

The abducted persons creating half-breeds from eggs taken from earth woman and fertilized by Reptoid men, create a half-breed that is masquerading as a Pleiadean humanoid and these entities are to interface between the Reptoids and the humans as being from the Pleiades and as being benevolent friends of humanity. This Awareness indicates that the establishment of their presence on earth along with government compliance is the intention of aliens, hoping that the government will cooperate with them on setting up a One World government in which they manipulate from behind the scenes the activities of the surface people, using them for slave labor or for work as needed and allowing them, the aliens, to have access to the human surface people according to their agenda: for food or for other purposes of their own needs. This Awareness indicates that the television miniseries "V," wich played early in the last decade, is a reasonably good attempt to portray the way by which these entities would seek to control the human masses on earth. The effort would be to control humans passively and to use force only when humans got out of line, or attempted to rebel" (R. of A., 1991-12, page 12).

"This Awareness indicates that It did not suggest that the Greys wanted to eradicate all of mankind; it suggested that they wanted control of the earth. Their purpose, their job, their reason for being here was to set up a One World Government to gain control over all human activities, using the humans to help control their own people, but also prepare the way for these others to follow, so that by the time they arrived, the human population would be under control. If, in gaining that control it is necessary to eradicate much of the population, that would be part of the action. This Awareness indicates that there are, for them, far more people on earth than they see as being necessary" (R. of A., 1990-11, page 9).

"This Awareness indicates that in regard to the Reptoids, the Greys are their servants. The human implants are the front-line of defense. The hybrid or half-breed children, half human/half Greys, are being taken elsewhere to be trained for military purposes, to be used as the second line of defense, therefore they will be fighting against humans, using technology available through the Reptoids, and the Greys will be behind these half-breeds, as the third line of defense. Finally, the fourth line of defense is the Reptoid civilization. This Awareness indicates that this generally is the situation as planned from their way of creating and preparing for any battle between earthlings and themselves; this in reference to the Reptoids' plan. This Awareness reminds you of earlier messages regarding the options available for humans. The options are a possible alliance with the Greys, and possible destruction of the Reptoid groups in their approach toward earth. That other options, of course, are to surrender or coexistence, which would be essentially an action of human sacrifice" (R. of A., 1992-2, page 14).

"This Awareness indicates that in reference to those who are seen human-like aliens; these have been reported as blonde and fair-skinned beings. There are the two types: that type which comes from the Pleiades - these entities being genuine highly evolved spiritual beings who would have liked to help humans; these being in part associated with the Intergalactic Confederation. The entity Semjase (made famous by Billy Meier) as being one such entity who has communicated to humans from this group. These entities are true friends to humans. There is also the other blonde fair-skinned types who work as subordinates to the Greys; these entities having been abducted or having been offspring of abductees, raised and trained by the Greys as servants, obey orders from the Greys. This reference is to the Greys, as being the Zeta Riticuli from the Bernard Star" (R. of A., 1990-6, page 9).

"The blonde Nordic types, many of these having been created on earth, are cloned in fact. Some of these are clones of the Reptoids and Greys. Others are the clones of the government, to serve purposes of the government" (Revelations of Awareness, 1993-5, page 8).

"This Awareness indicates that these entities (the aliens) think of themselves as custodians of humanity, much the way a farmer would see himself as a shepherd of sheep or one who owns cattle. This Awareness indicates that the aliens also occasionally refer to their role as 'handler,' especially in regard to the abduction of women, from whom they collect eggs for fertilization on a regular basis, each woman being assigned a particular handler" (R. of A. 1991-12, page 13).

"This Awareness indicates that the Reptoids are already on the planet and few see them. Some who have been abducted have reported seeing these very tall people standing in the background watching. Most of the time these are Reptoids; in some cases they may be those from Orion, the Orion Empire. The Reptoids generally are present with the short Greys in the ships. This Awareness indicates that it is the intention of the Reptoids not to engage directly in war with humans, but to have half-breeds and abductees involved in such, if war with humans erupts. It is the intention of the Reptoids not to engage directly in war with Pleiadians or those from Sirius who come in to rescue humanity, but to have the humans and the abductees and the half-breeds to carry on any war with those extraterrestrials from the Pleiades or from Sirius, if they enter into the affairs of Earthians. The Reptilians (they are so-called because they have a reptile genetic base) prefer to let others kill themselves off rather than get in the midst of direct conflict with their enemies, (Revelations of Awareness, 1991-12, page 13).

"This Awareness indicates....the Pleiadians' ships are different from the Greys and their appearance is different. Their symbol is that of a serpent climbing a vine, or of a serpent. The Reptilian symbol is that of a dragon. The Grey's symbol also uses a serpent, this being a cobra" (R. of A. 1990-10, page 19).

"This Awareness wishes entities to understand that there are three major players in the galaxy: the Reptoid Federation, the Galactic Confederation, and the Orion Empire. The Orion Empire as that which is ruled basically by one leader. The Reptoid Federation as that which is a conglomeration of many different groups, in which the Reptoids in various types of species have joined together, and the Galactic Confederation as that which is made up from federations of different star systems throughout the galaxy, these being mostly of the human types. In some cases the serpent, what is termed the serpent race, will be involved. This Awareness indicates the serpent race as that which was a sub-species from Draco, which broke away many eons ago, and has been aligned with the Galactic Confederation for some time. Their main home, as far as human knowledge is concerned, would be that of Sirius. There are many other places where these entities reside" (R. of A. 1991-16, page 6).

"This awareness indicates the New World Order is part of the alien agenda, promoted by those Greys from Orion. Their purpose is to set up the world for its future inclusion in the Orient Empire. This Awareness indicates that while this is planned, it is not seen as the only option or alternative. It is seen that the Galactic Confederation, which includes the Pleiadians and the Vegans and the Sirius groups, are all also concerned and hoping that earth does not become part of the Orion Empire, or the Draco Federation. This Awareness indicates that they prefer to see the earth become part of the Galactic Confderation....This Awareness indicates the Orion Greys (the tall big-nosed Greys) appear to be in a position of economic power, wherein they are more powerful economically, and thus hold control over other extraterrestrials, such as the Draconias and the Zeta Reticuli. This Awareness indicates the small Greys (or those of the Zeta Reticuli) are basically mercenaries under the domination of the Draco Reptiles, which in their turn are subservient to the Orion Greys, even though they have greater military power and greater force. The Draconian forces have the ability to take control away from the Orion Greys, but the Orion Greys are such good managers of planets that the Draco Reptoids do not envy them of their job and therefore, let themselves be the military arm of operation, while giving the economic and political control to the Orion forces....This Awareness indicates the Galactic Command, composed of the Pleiadians, Vegans, Sirius and Arcturians, is such that it keeps a low profile, because they have not been clearly invited by all of human representatives and governments to assist humans in throwing off the yoke of oppression that will come from these Draconians and Orion forces....The Galactic Command simply waits with its plans and abilities and forces until the time is right for it to move in order to help humanity, if indeed humanity does seek help" (R. of A., 1993-14, page 15).

"Once there is a New World Order, if it is indeed a tyranny, which appears to be the case, there is no force that will intervene to help throw off the tyrant except perhaps if it comes from some extraterrestrial source....If the One World Government is ever set up the way they want it to be, they will confiscate all weapons, and have them only in the hands of trusted and loyal militia. They will prevent all leaders from having a way of speaking out to rally the masses, into any kind of action, and they will generally keep tight control by making sure they have just enough to eat, just enough to live with, if they are obedient and work properly so as to not have too much time for mischief or for talking about overthrowing the government, or for any other kind of activity that is not related, or perhaps some amount of rest and recuperation from one's work. This Awareness indicates that it will not be an age of art and philosophy, for they will not allow free thinking or free art, any more than occurred in the Soviet Union. In fact, this will become even more stringent. The New World Government as proposed and as fitting to the alien agenda is designed mostly to make use of human energies for working and building the world into a suitable place for its masters: the extraterrestrial beings who intend to take over and run the place for their masters, and to keep humanity subservient and in labor for their purposes" (R. of A., 1993-14, page 17).

"This Awareness indicates that these entities (the aliens), by necessity and by their nature, look upon humans as inferior creators, capable of supplying them with some of their biological needs. They do not see humans as having any special divine rights to life, liberty or individuality. They see humans as simply being another type of animal on earth which has certain unique qualities in terms of its chemical make-up, in terms of hormones, in terms of various qualities that can be used to extract energy and life essence....this Awareness indicates that essentially, the activities of aliens are incompatible with the values of humans. This Awareness would also like to point out the aliens are very much aligned with the forces that are associated with Satan. This Awareness indicates that the Greys - the Orion Greys and the Reptoids are the ones this Awareness is speaking of at this time. The angelic hosts are associated with those of the Pleiadians, Sirius, Arcturian, Vegan forces. There are also others. This Awareness indicates that the demons that work with Satan are the higher officials in the ranks of the Reptoid and

Orion Greys. The Zeta Reticuli are simply little imps....This Awareness indicates that essentially, what you have in these negative extraterrestrials is the Satanic hierarchy, and what you have in the friendly extraterrestrials is like the angelic hosts as presented in the Christian doctrine" (R. of A., 1993–14, page 18).

"This Awareness indicates essentially, the souls of people are of greatest urgency to the Galactic Command or Confederation, for this saving of the souls is that which the spiritual forces perceive to be the real purpose and value. The physical body is temporal anyway, and has only a short time on earth. The soul being more permanent, being more or less eternal, is the more important concern. The Draconians and Orion forces think that by making it appear the soul is just an illusion and that one's body is what counts, will find themselves able to influence people by fear and by coercion, based on bodily needs and preservation. And in this manner they actually capture the souls of entities who are trying to preserve their body and will do so at the cost of their soul" (R. of A., 1993–14, page 20).

• • •

THE THIRD PROPHECY OF FATIMA IS ABOUT THE ALIEN AGENDA

"When this Awareness indicated the Third prophecy of Fatima as being a prophecy of nuclear war, this was not the full prophecy or full scenario of the prophecy. This Awareness indicates the alien factor as that which was such as to contribute to that nuclear war and it was in part the intention of aliens to bring about enough devastation so as to make the planet easily conquered, while still retaining a certain degree of lifeforms, whereby with certain technologies they could therefore then eliminate the radioactive contamination and inhabit the earth without any threat of human domination" (Revelations of awareness 1990-4, page 7).

"This Awareness indicates that if these Fatima Prophecy events occur on schedule you can expect a nuclear war or nuclear incident to occur in the Middle East....as a further part of the Fatima prophecies, after which, the aliens would then be able to make their appearance as though they were some intruding gods coming in to straighten out the mess that humans had created. This essentially is the skeletal overview of the alien agenda; along with the incoming planet which some refer to as the '12th Planet' carrying the warriors for the alien takeover at that time, to comprise the high points of the alien agenda" (Revelations of Awareness 1992-4, page 12).

Was Nostradamus referring also to those invading aliens when he wrote in his quatrain No. 72, from century No. 10: **"On the seventh month of the year 1999,/A great king of terror will come from the sky"?**

"This Awareness indicates that there are other systems that contribute to this galactic effort to free the earth and similar planets from domination by the Orion Empire and the Reptoids and the Greys, since these types generally end up enslaving the masses on the planets, and the Galactic Confederation prefers to see planets that are more or less free from slavery. These then, when free from slavery, tend to be more inclined to trading with the Galactic Confederation and to further the commercial activities of the planet so that free travel and trade without conflict becomes available in regard to that planet (R. of A. 1992-9, page 10).

This Awareness indicates that in regard to the Pleideans, Vegans, Arcturians and Sirius forces, all of which are allies with each other; these entities have long held back and watched for fear that they might interfere with the Prime Directive which they follow and which has been stated in the Star Trek series as interfering with a planet's own culture and evoluntionary interests.

They do not wish to interfere with that which is the wish of a people on a planet. They have held back because the leaders on earth have up to this time not been open or receptive to speaking with or discussions aligning the Pleideans and their allies.

The Greys and the Reptoids had their own agenda for earth and made certain contacts and contacts with earth leaders. It was only in the past few months that the forces from the allied groups became aware of the discrepancy between the leaders of the world's nations and the people of the world, whereby they realized that the leaders of many of these nations were working not as representatives of the people but as manipulators of their own people, and that they were working to manipulate on behalf of the Greys and the Reptoids.

This allowed them to take a new look at the rules by which they adhere in regard to that which is called the Prime Directive of non-interference. They realized that they not only had a right to interfere, but an obligation when a leader of a country is manipulating the masses rather than representing the masses. This Awareness indicates that it is for this reason that these entities are making strong moves at this time, to make their presence known and to give the people of the world great choice, a greater chance for throwing off the yoke of oppression. (R. of A. 1994-9, page 10).

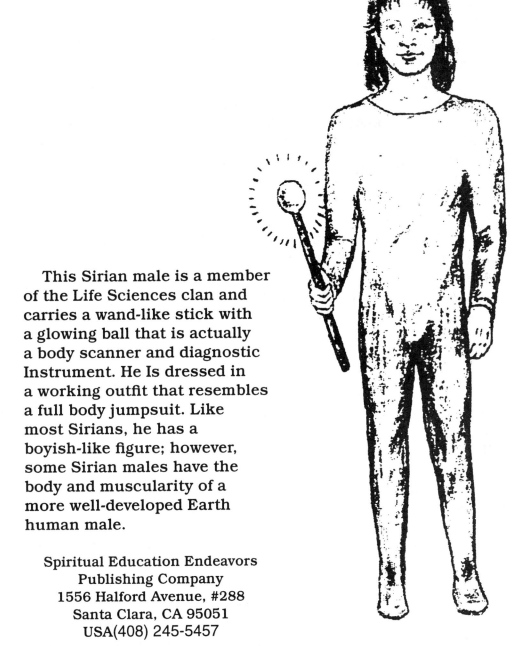

This Sirian male is a member of the Life Sciences clan and carries a wand-like stick with a glowing ball that is actually a body scanner and diagnostic Instrument. He Is dressed in a working outfit that resembles a full body jumpsuit. Like most Sirians, he has a boyish-like figure; however, some Sirian males have the body and muscularity of a more well-developed Earth human male.

Spiritual Education Endeavors
Publishing Company
1556 Halford Avenue, #288
Santa Clara, CA 95051
USA(408) 245-5457

Typical Sirian Male

From the book: "You are Becoming A Galactic Human," 1994, by Virginia Essene and Sheldon Nidle, S.E.E. Publishing Co., with permission.

• • •

In TIME magazine of May 23, 1994, James Reston Jr. said that Shoemaker-Levy 9 was orbiting Jupiter rather than following the more usual cometary path around the sun, he added: "This phantom, which seemed to have the trademark of coments...Indeed a unique object, different from other cometary forms....The object, if it was an object and not some errant ghost image, was unique."

Moreover, Shoemaker-Levy started fragmenting similar to a layered pancakes, from five to 17 and finally to 21 individual nuclei, all in a neatly perfect line and all of roughly equivalent size.

Cosmic Awareness indicated that comets are composed of ice, and these particles [of Shoemaker-Levy] were not ice, but rock or solid material for the most part; and that anyone knows that chunks of a comet or asteroids do not move in lines, in a formation of the type observed. Awareness has identified those "cometary fragments" as Reptoid spacecrafts.

"This Awareness indicates these so-called asteroids [Shoemaker-Levy train] as part of a planetoid that contained Reptoid aliens who were in deep-freeze heading toward earth, after a planned loop near Jupiter....that the planetoid was made to split apart on its approach toward Jupiter, creating these various rock particles [the fragments of Shoemaker-Levy]....This Awareness indicates that the planetoid being blasted apart from within itself as part of a plan by the Reptoids in its own operative strategy to allow the separate particles to move individually on their own, following signals from the guiding craft/particle in the lead. Those signals were distorted in order for the guiding craft at the front of the formation to crash into Jupiter.... so that the other ships being guided by that same navigational beam, would follow suit...they simply followed each other into the planet and crashed. This Awareness indicates that during their stupor, sleep or slow thawing process, they were not able to think about what to do. They were simply being guided mechanically and electronically by devices aboard the ships, particularly the leading ship.

This awareness indicates that this is a great setback for the New World Order, for the NWO was a plan by and for the Reptoids, and it (the NWO) would have benefited greatly had the Reptoids made their invasion on earth. It would have led to the need for a New World Order.

"This Awareness indicates the Reptoids on earth presently are individually powerful, but do not have great numbers to be able to conquer humanity, and therefore, their threat is highly diminished." (Revelations of Awareness, issue No. 439, 1994-13, from a reading given on August 8, 1994).

A picture released by NASA of the invading Reptoid space fleet (Shoemaker-Levy 9) as recorded by The Hubble Space Telescope on January 1994.

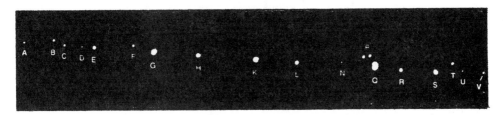

Awareness indicated that the interrupting force that threw the Reptoid fleet off course may have well been one of the groups (the Pleiadeans, lyraians, Vegans, Arcturians or Syrians) who are officially at war with the Draconians or the Reptoids.

A detail of a drawing by the artist Jon Strongbow showing Reptoid ships, camouflaged by the use of rocks and dust as asteroids, crashing into Jupiter.

• • • • • •

Recently a tailles "comet" has been discovered, named for its discoverers the Hale-Bopp comet. This object or planet is heading toward our solar system from the direction of Sagittarius. Its due to arrive in 1997, and come close to earth in 1999.

In an Oct. 24, 1995 reading, Awareness indicated: "It does appear that this is very much the same as what was described by Zecharia Sitchin (as the Twelfth Planet) and that it is inhabited by Reptoids in a frozen state. It appears to be that which was connected with the previous 'comet' that plowed into Jupiter which had served as an advance ship of these entities.

"This appears to be the main body of the military group of Reptoids. However, because the first contingent contained the leaders, this group will be much more in a state of disarray and confusion if they are successful in approaching earth. It appears there will be an interception prior to their entry into the earth's orbit. It is seen also that they may be deflected in a different direction before approaching the earth itself. There is nothing clear or certain at this time."

A reading from Paul Solomon Source tells about a red planet coming close to earth and abruptly tilting the poles: "As there is the passing close of that red planet, so will the crust of the earth be attracted toward it, the North Pole pointing in the direction of its advance or approach. And when it is at its nearest point to earth, the N.P. will point directly upward or in that direction (the same direction of now or near). And in its passing away from earth the poles would tilt again a third time toward the opposite direction; consequently there will be three separate temperature changes, making near to impossible the survival of any animal species or plant upon the most of the surface of planet earth."

• • • • • •

ELOHIM CREATED THE PROTOTYPE HUMANS

"This Awareness indicates that humans were created by the Elohim [the Elohim are highly advanced and evolved human-like entities]....the humans have within them a certain type of genetic cellular code that allows them from generation to generation to develop and evolve toward Godhead or Godhood. This Awareness indicates that this is lacking in the Greys....the Elohim were the true creators of the human types, including the Pleiadeans, the Andromedeans and the humans....The Elohim types were the founders or fathers or creators of the human and Pleiadean beings" (Revelations of Awareness, 1992–2).

In other readings, Awareness indicated that Jesus Christ was an Elohim.

"This Awareness indicates that the brain was genetically engineered for humans, for their full potential. They have not yet reached that full potential. It is that coding, that secret coding that the Sirius engineers implanted in the human, that has helped them to grow, generation after generation, very quickly, to become a challenge to the Zeta Reticuli, and the Reptilian race. The humans being only about 12,000 years old in their present state, as Homo Sapiens, have developed at an enormously quick pace, in comparison to the development of the Zeta Reticuli who are over a half-million years old, or the Reptilians who are some 5 million years old.

"This Awareness indicates that the potential of the human brain to become ten times more powerful than it presently is, is seen by the Reptilians and the Zeta Reticuli as danger, a threat to them. The code given by the Sirius genetic engineers, in their part in the creation of the human creation as that which has allowed for humans to evolve to gain God-like powers in a very short time. They become individualistic which is beyond the understanding of the Zeta Reticuli, who must follow rules and act as a hive in their thinking. The humans also have the ability to intuitively or physically perceive and see things that are not based strictly on the five senses, and the perception that accompanies their senses.

"The Zeta Reticuli have what appears to be telepathy, where they can communicate telepathically, but this can be done through the use of their implants. They are not highly evolved, even though they are half a million years old....This Awareness indicates you have invisible deities, invisible angels protecting you, observing you, guiding you....These Zeta Reticuli are without souls. You have a soul. You have an astral body. You have a spirit body. You have God potential. The body itself, the physical body, is but one of many of your bodies...." (Revelations of Awareness, 1991–17, page 3).

THE MYSTERY OF ABDUCTIONS BY NEGATIVE ALIENS

"This Awareness indicates that the Greys that entities refer to as the Zeta Reticuli, the short small Greys, the cute little ones who appear to work for the tall blondes, are in fact working for the Reptilians as a kind of mercenary hired types, forerunners, who were set out ahead to set the stage for the Reptilian masters. Those who are often seen in abduction situations as tall humans with blonde hair are in fact half-breeds wearing wigs; that they often claim themselves to be Pleiadeans when in fact they are half-breeds from the Reptilian/human genetic engineering experiments; that in most cases they are from test-tube type formation from egg and sperm combination, from the human and the Reptilians. This awareness indicates their motives in abducting at this time in taking eggs from the human woman, as related to the effort to build an army of half-breeds to be used in the future in the event of war or in the event of needing these half-breeds to interface with the human race. The human race is of such a nature as to have a subconscious abhorrence to the Reptilians, due in part to a genetic recollection of the terrible

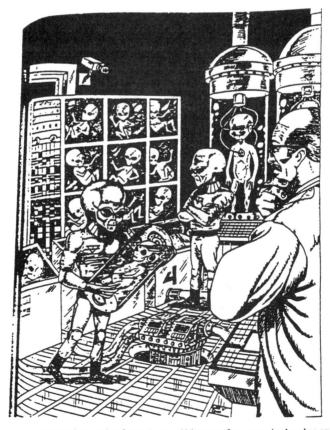

Depiction by an artist of an underground laboratory of a grey species, based on several eyewitness accounts of abductees. From *Matrix II: The Abduction and Manipulation of Human Beings Using Advanced Technology*, 1989/90, By Valdamar Valerian, Leading Edge Research Group, P.O. Box 7530, Yelm, Washington 98597. With Permission.

treatment the Reptilians once gave toward humans, and due in part to cultural training which conditions entities to think of reptiles as associated with evil. These entities therefore perceive the value in having half-breeds to work between themselves and humans.

"This Awareness indicates that the abductions at this time are not to preserve the humans race as it is, but to create a new race that will be able to serve the Reptilians in their needs, that will be more obedient to the Reptilians, for humans have individualistic quality which has evolved over the years, over the generations, which makes them extremely difficult to control by these Reptilians....This Awareness indicates that the Reptilians do eat humans, the way humans eat chicken. (The sweet and tender human flesh being a delicacy to them.) The Grey do tell stories to make entities feel comfortable with their actions....This Awareness indicates that humans have a kind of inborn or inbred compassion that requires effort to overcome, whereas the Greys tend to lack any such compassion at all.

"This Awareness indicates that essentially, the book **The Watchers**, has good abduction stories that are based in fact. The conclusion that the Greys are benign is that which does not recognize much of the reality of their purpose and mission. It simply buys in to the impression that the Greys want to create. It is in their interest to promote such feelings by those who have been abducted, and many of those who have been abducted believe that they have been privileged, and believe that their abduction is for some higher spiritual purpose, for the good of humanity....This Awareness indicates that until recently, when the half-breeds were successful as an experiment, the Greys were attempting various experiments using sperms and eggs to see if there was a possibility of reintroducing a combination of a human/Grey type being that would take the best of both kinds to extend their own species. These experiments were unsuccessful. Their effort to clone themselves with human genetics have not been as satisfactory as those using the Reptilian or Reptoid genes and humans. This Awareness indicates that much of this is what is actually behind the majority of abductions; the experiments in trying to commingle and create a new race, drawing from the genes of Reptoids and humans. This Awareness indicates that this has its roots back as far as forty thousand years in the past, at the beginning of the homo sapiens types, and also that there have been subsequent experiments with various types of races. There has also been some confusion and curiosity in regard to the nature of the human genetics because they grew to be different from the original homo sapiens; the evolution of the humans race becoming much more accelerated than was expected by those who were involved in the production of the species" (R. of A., 1991-9, page 11).

"This awareness indicates the Greys did not, even though they claimed they did, did not create the human beings, or the homo sapiens. There are some references implying such, there are some claims by the Greys as to having done so. They did influence some of the earlier evolutionary species of humans, but the more recent homo sapiens were the product of those beings of the human type, the more human type of beings. It is they who created the sex drive; this as referring to the human-type Elohim (by whom the Pleiadeans, those from Sirius, and the earth humans were created). The Greys have created other types of creatures. This Awareness indicates that the sex drive of humans is that which was intended to create a large population. It was during the early history that the war between the Pleiadeans and the Greys became pronounced on this plane, which led to the Pleiadeans' loss of the dominion over earth, and left the Greys who were the underground deities from Orion, left them having greater influence on the earth plane" (R. of A., 1991-2, page 10).

"There are many humans in the past who worshipped the Reptoid types and many will again do so, or they may worship the half-breeds, thinking the half-breeds are a superior race, worthy of worship" (R. of A., 1991-9, page 13).

"The aliens prefer to pretend, particularly the Grey aliens, to be gods and to have humans worship them as gods, and when this can be accomplished, they like to keep their human followers in the position of worshipping them as some kind of idol-type being" (R. of A., 1992-9, page 10).

In a reading on January 1994, Awareness indicated again that "the aliens enjoy having entities worship them. It is not that this is a major role of their part, but they do enjoy it when entities think of them as some kind of Divine being or messenger of God, because it makes it easier for them to manipulate the entity and get cooperation from the entity."

In another reading Awareness indicated that "these aliens do not care to share their target victims [the abducted and implanted ones] with spiritual orientation; they want them to worship them exclusively. This Awareness suggests therefore, to surround yourself with those meditations, prayers, icons, symbols of a religious nature, and meditate on spiritual things and keep yourself oriented to the spiritual aspects of life and see these entities as other than your friend. This Awareness indicates that these entities have the ability to transcend dimensions, come from one dimension into your dimension, or return to their other dimension that parallels [is similar] to this, but they can only do this and only interfere with you if you allow it, and if no spiritual energies prevent them from entering and having an effect upon you" (R. of A. 1992-7, page 4).

"This Awareness indicates that the aliens, this especially in reference to the negative aliens, those who are mostly associated with the Zeta Reticuli and the Orion Greys, do not care to have close contact with truly spiritual beings. They would like to divert spiritual beings from their spiritual path if possible, but they do not care to engage in any meaningful conflict or contact with these entities because they sense that the spiritual beings can see through them and know them for what they are. Essentially, many of these entities are representatives of a non-spiritual force associated with the Asuras [demons] spoken of by Rudolph Steiner; that these are very materialistic and non-compassionate beings whose interest lies mostly in self-perpetuation and the use of power and who see humans as much likened unto cattle. They are to be used. This Awareness indicates they do understand that humans have certain very unusual and special qualities which frighten them. It is this spiritual power that some humans have that is intriguing and frightening to them....Therefore, the aliens are quite apprehensive about dealing with entities who have strong spiritual souls, and tend to stay away from them. They are generally apprehensive of any contacts with such entities; thus they are not likely to bother the spiritually strong individual. This Awareness indicates that if the spiritual entity goes through a period of weakness or a period of his life in which the spiritual energy is depleted or drained or lacking, during such times, these entities might have some opportunity of contact and attempt to throw the entity off his or her spiritual path, but as long as the entity embraces a strong spiritual direction and purpose on his or her life, they tend to stay clear of that energy.

"This Awareness wishes to make another point clear; religion is not the issue here. Spiritual energy is what this Awareness speaks of, and spiritual energy is enhanced by compassion and caring of the soul for others, and the love of the Divine and the association and integration of the soul with those higher Divine Forces. It does not mean the mouthing of slogans of a religious nature or the repetition of certain phrases or names associated with a religious belief. This is not the same as spirituality. There are many entities who spout Biblical scripture and who think that this is spirituality, while they continue to do misdeeds and unforgivable actions to their fellow humans, even in the name of their religion; that this kind of verbal religion as opposed to the spiritual religion is not true spirituality. It is but words and the garments of false religion.

"This Awareness indicates that this does not ward off aliens, in fact they are often attracted to this kind of entity who is a believer in terms of words and who spouts religious words, for these entities are often easy to convert. The alien will simply inform them that they are messengers from the entity's god and their purpose is to do certain things on earth and the entity will quickly turn and worship the alien, which is what they enjoy, for when they are worshipped, the entities usually will do whatever they direct them to do. They become very easily manipulated by the aliens at that point. The aliens can control those who mouth religion, and they do not mind working with these entities. This Awareness suggest therefore, those who wish to avoid being manipulated by aliens need to develop true spiritual energies in their lives and these spiritual energies, in which the Divine Forces of the universe are upper-most to the entity, these spiritual energies will protect entities from the aliens" (Revelations of Awareness, 1992-11, page 10).

A drawing of a tall grey from a particular subspecies/species of grey—the orion grey type 1. From "Matrix II," Leading Edge Research Group, P.O. Box 7530, Yelm, WA 98597. With permission.

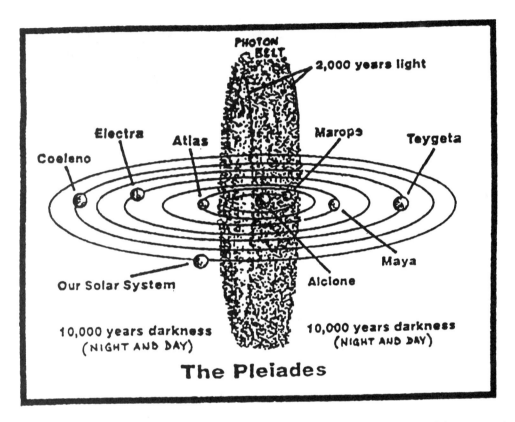

The Pleiades

Every 25,000 years our solar system completes one orbit around Alcione, the central sun of Pleiades, a constellation at a distance of approximately 400 light years from our sun. In 1961, science discovered a photon belt which encircles the Pleiades at a right angle to its orbital planes. Our sun, and earth with it, is entering this photon belt between now and the year 2012.

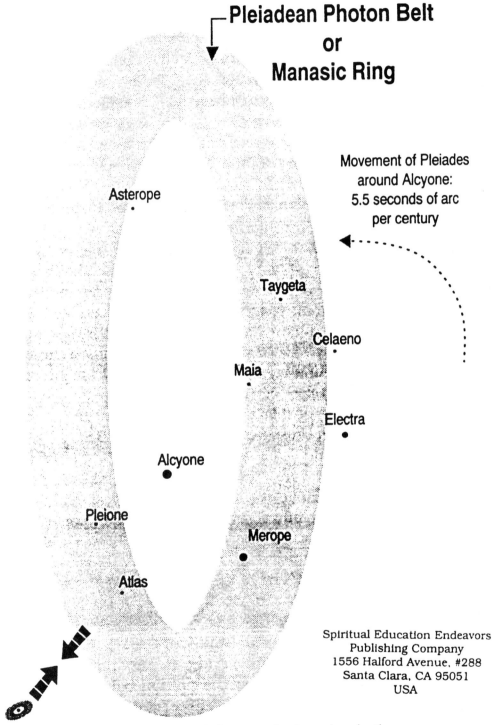

Pleiadean Photon Belt
or
Manasic Ring

Movement of Pleiades
around Alcyone:
5.5 seconds of arc
per century

Asterope

Taygeta

Celaeno

Maia

Electra

Alcyone

Pleione

Merope

Atlas

Spiritual Education Endeavors
Publishing Company
1556 Halford Avenue, #288
Santa Clara, CA 95051
USA

Your solar system and the photon belt are moving toward each other.

From the book: "You are Becoming A Galactic Human," 1994, by Virginia Essene and Sheldon Nidle, S.E.E. Publishing Co., with permission.

• • •

SUPPLEMENT 2

THE RAPTURE—INTO THE PHOTON BELT

The book *You Are Becoming A Galactic Human* by Virginia Essene and Sheldon Nidle, 1994, Published by Spiritual Education Endeavors (1556 Halford Avenue, #288, Santa Clara, CA 95051, USA), relates—a summary of the main points follows—that "our solar system is presently poised to enter a vast region of light called the photon belt. This huge mass of light will be the vehicle for our restoration to full consciousness and for the complete transformation of our DNA. These unbelievable changes will forever alter not only ourselves, but also our planet and our solar system. This is because the photon belt will move our solar system into a higher dimension (from 3rd to the 5th), allowing our planet, within the solar system, to move to a new position in space closer to the Sirius star system.

"The photon belt is a huge torroid shaped object (with a thickness of approximately 2000 solar years) composed of photon light particles. Those particles are the result of a collision between an anti-electron and an electron. This split-second collision causes the two particles to destroy each other. The resulting mass of this collision is completely converted into energy that register as photons or light particles. This photon energy will be the major source for all of our energy requirements in the future.

"As Earth is now going to enter this photon belt, it may now appear to be either the prelude to a new wondrous age or the time of our extinction.

"The photon belt can be divided into three sections. First we will enter through what is called the null zone. This procedure will take roughly five to six days to complete including approximately three days of total darkness. (Before entering the null zone we should expect a change in Earth's electrical, magnetic, and gravitational fields). Following this action, we will move into the main part of the belt itself and experience unending daylight. This journey normally lasts around 2000 years and ends when our solar system exits at the other end of the belt. However, in this cycle, our planet will not exists at the other end, because God has arranged for our solar system to enter an interdimensional rescue bubble, which is put by the Sirians inside the belt, and this bubble will thrust our solar system out of the photon belt through the 5th dimension and into a position about three light years from the Sirius star system.

"This shifting from a largely 3rd-dimensional world to a 5th dimensional world is an enormous gift, because as a result of this change we will be removed from Pleiadean control [the rule of the Law], and situated under Sirian influences [the rule of love and grace]. This 5th-dimensional reality means that we will be nearer to Sirius—that we can adopt the Lyran/Sirian culture and be under the protection of Sirius."

"Because of the immense electrical and consciousness changes all humans must undergo, the Galactic Confederation intends to orchestrate a mass landing of counselors, other personnel, and important scientific and healing technologies—up to six months before the photon belt arrives. They will tell us what is about to happen as well as how these changes are going to affect us."

"Planet Earth was granted full membership in the Galactic Confederation on March 5, 1993. This allowed the Galactic Confederation to legally establish its rescue mission and formally empower the First Contact Team to prepare its protocols for first contact and landing on Earth.

"The approaching photon belt will mark the end of our present civilization as we know....and our society is approaching an almost indescribable Golden Age that various Earth religious prophecies have forecast over the past 2000 years."

Since 1992, Cosmic Awareness also has been giving detailed information about this coming Photon Age. Selected excerpts from Its indications follow:

"This Awareness indicated that there is energy of a belt that is in the path of the movement of the solar system, and it may be referred to as a photon belt or belt of light. This is more as a kind of spiritual energy, as a kind of Liquid Light that affects consciousness. For those who have a consciousness that can adjust to higher frequencies of love and light it will be a time of blissful joy. For those who are embittered, hostile and greedy and very grounded in negative energies, it will be a time in which they experience great weakening."

"In general, it appears that the earth is moving toward a field of energy which is called the photon belt, and that this field of energy can and will have a profound effect on the energies of the electromagnetic field on earth and that entities will have an opportunity to be altered genetically because of the electromagnetic change on their bodies and the light photons that will affect them, even to the cellular levels of the human body."

"This Awareness indicates that those entities who are incapable of moving into these higher frequencies because of their own lower density will find it extremely difficult to maintain a sense of individuality, and if they can and do choose to keep their individualities based on lower frequencies, they will eventually have an experience of being outcast from these energy fields and movements into a lower dimension."

"This Awareness indicates the information about the people from Sirius is correct. This is one reason why these entities (the Sirians) do not become excessively concerned at the efforts of the Greys and the Reptoids to enslave humanity, for they recognize that there is a greater change following soon that will put all of this to nothing, and that the controls that the Reptoids and Greys so dearly seek on the earth will be meaningless. This Awareness indicates that those who cooperate with the Reptoids, with the Greys on these efforts to enslave humanity, will be moving also into this photon zone, and will be caught in a kind of mental warp that puts them into their own private hell or private prison within that mind-scape or consciousness-scape that replaces the landscape of earth, for as these entities move into their dream state (the new dimension) it becomes likened unto their own private nightmare."

"These Awareness indicates the New World Order planners are concerned about keeping the approach of the photon belt secret in order to gain the most possible advantage from anything that occurs. They see the photon belt as a natural phenomenon that they can take advantage of and lead the masses into a subservient position while they set up controls all over the planet. The only thing is, they are not taking into account the presence of the Sirians landing, wherein the Sirians may supersede the power of the New World Order promoters."

"This Awareness indicates that many of the plans of the negative aliens and those who support them may find themselves taking over a world which becomes another dying planet for them."

"This Awareness indicates that huge numbers of extraterrestrial and inter-dimensional beings are watching earth because it is such a unique experiment, to have evolution move so quickly."

"This Awareness indicates that it appears more than one photon belt is being created in this galaxy; that the purpose of this is to move certain planets, rearrange places and re-establish a clearer order for the Galactic Confederation and its alliances. Also, this is used for moving planets into higher frequencies or dimensions. This is being done with the efforts of a great number of beings, not limited to the Sirians or even entities in this galaxy alone; that there appears to be some help from the Andromeda galaxy on this also, and others.

"The Sirians appear to be working with the earth and the more localized photon belt, but others appear to be doing similar activities in other parts of the galaxy. Much of this is to defuse the efforts of the Draconians, Orion and other negative beings who have been trying to take control of certain galaxies and planets and solar systems and star systems."

"This Awareness indicates that it appears that this is a kind of cosmic connection between this solar system and the Sirius star system that has been since the creation of this galaxy; that has always been part of the galactic behavior. This Awareness indicates it is seen as a connective relationship between the star system Sirius and the solar system, in the same way that a parent and a child, or man and wife have a connection. There is a cosmic connection between these two, energy-wise, and the photon belt is a kind of carrier in the process of the merging between these energy groups."

"This Awareness indicates that there is a question also in the timing. To project when the events will begin is somewhat difficult. It will be more likely that it is a growing thing rather than a sudden change that occurs, and the growing thing may begin in the mid-Nineties, but may take considerable amount of time before it reaches a point of completion. This Awareness does not refer by 'completion' to the end of the experience, but rather to the complete transition into the total experience, and this Awareness has projected the time to be approximately 2012 or 2013, when this experience will be entered into fully."

"It is seen that the Sirians will come (will land) and prepare humans on earth for the movement into the photon belt, and that they would remain on earth as it moved through the null zone and into the photon belt."

"The effect of Sirian technology is to help guide the movement of the solar system as it enters the Photon Belt, using certain photon energies and technologies available to the Sirians as they help to veer the solar system in its movement so that it comes closer to the Sirian star system than normally would have occurred."

"The Sirians have some capacity for moving energies and appear to be able to use certain energies within the Photon Belt to allow new energies in the solar system to be influenced by the photons in such a way as to help align the earth and Sirius—help align the solar system and Sirius in a certain maneuver based partly on the use of energies that are already present.

"There will be a slight deviation in the normal orbiting path of the solar system for it to come together with Sirius but in general, Sirius and earth tend to converge because of the Photon Belt and this converging is generally a natural occurring event with some slight assistance from the Sirian technology that has been developed in recent times to help bring that convergence into a closer harmony than would naturally have occurred.

"The main contribution of Sirian technology to the solar system is that of assisting the planet's life forms to accept and adapt to the new energies that will be part of the Photon Belt influence on the atmosphere of the earth particularly as it will disrupt any types of polarized electrical fields, neutralizing these electrical fields.

"The Sirians will help bring the new photon energy into focus and help reestablish energies and energy technologies and applications for replacing the electrical objects commonly used on earth. Some of the old electrical appliances will be still usable, but the energy that powers them will come from Photon energies and devices. Other electrical devices will have to be scrapped as they will no longer be of any value."

"This Awareness indicates that essentially the people from Sirius are cousins to humankind. They are also in part responsible for the modern version of humanity."

"This Awareness indicates that entities should cherish their life at this time, for its unique opportunity to be part of this great event that is occurring in the universe, on this earth, and recognize that even though there will be some pain and suffering involved in experiencing these enormous changes, you are extremely fortunate to be part of such an event, and if you move through these frequencies and vibrational changes without mental disruption or resentment or repression or trying to avoid what can't be avoided, you will have a much easier transition from this dimension to the next."

A CHRISTIAN VIEWPOINT OF THE PHOTON AGE

The Bible says that very soon Jesus will return "in the clouds with power and great majesty," to rescue all of His children, (Matthew 24:29–31), and remake the Earth into a beautiful New Earth. Everybody who loves Jesus will then receive a wonderful new super-body. In our new heavenly super-bodies we will be able to fly through the sky freer than the birds, and will never again feel weariness, sickness, hunger nor pain; but will enjoy heavenly happiness, unending adventures and beautiful pleasures with the Lord and each other forever.

Have you "come to Jesus?" If so, He will come into you—Into your heart to forgive you for all of the wrong that you have ever done and to give you His free gift of eternal life. You can receive Jesus' love and forgiveness right now by saying this little prayer:

"Dear Jesus, please forgive me for being bad. Thank you so much for dying for my sins. I now ask You, dear Jesus, to please come into my heart and give me Your free gift of eternal heavenly life—Help me to love you, read Your Word and try to help others to know You also, in Jesus' name I pray, amen!"

"Then Jesus Christ will command His angels, by a special act of His Justice and Mercy, to deliver all His enemies to death. Then suddenly all persecutors of the Church of Jesus Christ and all evil doers will perish, and rest and peace between God and man will appear. Jesus Christ will be served, adored, and glorified" (from La Salette Prophecy of Mother Mary).

Epilogue

THE HOPE

● ● ● ● ● ● ● ● ● ● ● ● ● ●

THE REFUGE

He who dwells in the shelter of the Most High will abide in the shadow of the Almighty.

I will say to the Lord, "My refuge and my fortress, My God, in whom I trust!"

For it is He who delivers you from the snare of the trapper, and from the deadly pestilence.

He will cover you with His pinions, and under His wings you may seek refuge.

His faithfulness is a shield and bulwark. You will not be afraid of the terror by night, or of the arrow that flies by day; of the pestilence that stalks in darkness, or of the destruction that lays waste at noon.

A thousand may fall at your side, and ten thousand at your right hand; but it shall not approach you.

You will only look on with your eyes, and see the recompense of the wicked. For you have made the Lord your refuge, even the Most High, your dwelling place.

No evil will befall you, nor will any plague come near your tent. For He will give His angels charge concerning you, to guard you in all your ways (from Psalm 91).

A PRAYER

Jesus is the Way, the Truth, and the Light. Those who come to Christ Jesus shall not perish, because He will raise them up in these historic days we are living in and give them everlasting life.

Jesus said: "For what does it profit a man to gain the whole world, and forfeit his soul? For what shall a man give in exchange for his soul?" (Mark 8:36, 37).

In order to become reconciled with God, the uttering with faith of the following prayer is necessary:

"My Lord and my God, have mercy upon my soul, a sinner. I believe that Jesus Christ is the Son of the living God. I believe that he died on the cross and shed His blood for the forgiveness of all my sins. I believe

151

that God raised Jesus from the dead by the power of the Holy Ghost. I open up the door of my heart and I invite you into my heart, Lord Jesus. Wash all of my sins away in the precious blood that you shed for me. O Jesus, come into my heart. I bid you enter my whole temple now. By my free will I welcome you, and I let go of everything. O Jesus, my Lord, receive me as your own, and I thank you for saving my soul."

GOD IS LOVE

Man's spiritual nature is represented by a diagram known as "The Chart of the Divine Self." There are three figures represented in the chart. The upper figure, surrounded by spheres of light, is the presence of God that dwells with man; the I AM Presence; the I AM THAT I AM; the individualization of God's presence for every son and daughter of the Most High. The middle figure is Christ, the Mediator between God and man, called the Holy Christ Self. This Inner Teacher overshadows the lower self, which consists of the soul evolving through the four planes of Matter using the vehicles of the four lower bodies: Etheric, mental, emotional and physical bodies.

The three figures correspond to the Trinity of Father (the upper figure), Son (the middle figure), and Holy Spirit (the lower figure). The latter is the intended temple of the Holy Spirit. The soul in the lower figure is the non-permanent aspect of being which is made permanent through the process of ascension—whereby the soul merges first with the Holy Christ Self and then with the living Presence of the I AM THAT I AM. Once the ascension has taken place, the soul, the non-permanent aspect of being, becomes the Incorruptible One, a permanent atom in the Body of God. The Chart of the Divine Self is therefore a diagram of one's past, present, and future.

The threefold flame of life is the divine spark sent from the I AM Presence and sealed in the secret chamber of the heart. Also called the Christ flame and the liberty flame, or fleur-de-lis, it is the spark of a man's Divinity, his potential for Christhood.

The silver or crystal cord is the stream of life that descends from the heart of the I AM Presence to the Holy Christ Self to nourish and sustain the soul and its vehicles of expression in time and space.

The dove of the Holy Spirit descending from the heart of the Father is shown just above the head of the Christ. When the son of man puts on and becomes the Christ consciousness as Jesus did, he merges with the Holy Christ Self. The Holy Spirit is upon him and the words of the Father, the beloved I AM Presence, are spoken, "This is my beloved Son in whom I AM well pleased" (Matthew 3:17).

(The visual concepts in the chart date back to the I AM Activity, founded in 1931, but the principles go back to Jesus and before).

The Chart and the Text: Courtesy of Summit University Press

THE ALIEN SITUATION: AN UPDATE

(From an AWARENESS reading given on Sept. 9, 1995)

This Awareness indicates that the Zeta aliens are hired and controlled by the Reptoids, who in turn are subservient to those from Orion. The Orion group tends to control the empire through economic controls with the Reptoids having the greater military force, and the Zeta Reticuli being subservient, serving as a kind of mercenary army under the Reptoids.

The Zeta, who have set up their civilization on earth, have several groups, some of which are inclined to work with humans against the Reptoids because they find humans to be better, more benevolent masters than the Reptoids. The humans who work with the Zeta tend to have a relationship that is relatively friendly.

The motive of the friendship is to gain technology from the Zeta Reticuli. The humans are not enthusiastic about the presence of the Reptoids on the planet, and many efforts have been made to have help from the Zeta in ridding the planet of the Reptoids, if it can be accomplished without too much risk.

This Awareness indicates that not too much has been changed since previous updates. Essentially, the Zeta Reticuli are still in place, mostly in their underground civilizations. The Reptoids have been relatively calm and are in a state of quite uncertainty after their comrades crashed into Jupiter. (See page 135).

This Awareness indicates that the Zeta Reticuli appear to be in a kind of routine in which they are focusing more and more of the energy into working with human DNA to restore their own race to a more independent nature, whereby they can re-establish their reproductive capacity.

The cloning process which is used for reproducing the Zeta Reticuli is still being used, but greater advances in mixing of humans and Zeta Reticuli genetics is beginning to help the Zetas to reproduce through the normal sexual process of reproduction.

Particularly effective in this sense is through the Zeta females. They are gradually becoming more capable, through the use of genetic engineering, of having sexual relationship. Many encounters with humans along this line have helped them to become more able to have such relationships and there have been rare occasions in which the Zeta have given birth.

The effects have not been satisfactory. The birth process has produced weak children, but this is still a major breakthrough for them in that the birth of children through the female Zeta Reticuli is relatively new phenomenon.

This Awareness indicates that the abduction of humans for these genetic experiments and for cross-breeding attempts continues to occur, but there is a greater caution involved, wherein the violations are not so blatant as they were two years ago. Two years ago, people were being abducted and experiments were being done on the people with such a haste that there was much hardship on people abducted. It was as though there was a desperate need to get more and more material from humans for DNA experimentation. This rush is no longer quite so urgent.

The Zeta types are not so urgent in their rush to complete their work and this allows for more patience in dealing with the generic engineering process so that the abductees are treated with more respect, or patience, so that the experience is not so difficult for them.

This Awareness indicates that part of the reason for the extreme rush that was occurring was prompted by the recognition that the Reptoids were intending to impose their controls on the earth and the Zeta wanted to attend their own agenda prior to the Reptoids' arrival. There now is no longer seen a need for such urgency on their part.

• • •

This Awareness indicates that the [1947 Alien] autopsy was authentic in the film shown. Those that crashed at Roswell in 1947 were associated with Orion and were different types from the small Zeta Reticuli who did not arrive on earth until the early sixties. The female in the film "Alien Autopsy" is less dark in terms of greyness than many other tall Greys that have been described as big-nosed Greys, and the fact that she had no navel suggest that she had been cloned.

• • •

This Awareness wishes to remind you of certain prophecies by Nostradamus wherein a war starts in the Middle East and quickly spreads to Europe, particularly in the countries along the Mediterranean. This Awareness indicates that this is very dangerous situation that could get totally out of control. The Moslems are not likely to be of help to the New World Order, but they may help to set the stage, where the NWO could be implemented in other parts of the world to garner forces from other countries to come in and help Europe fight off the Moslems. This is seen as a situation that needs to be watched if it progresses further, for it could indeed become a very dangerous situation.

• • •

(For more AWARENESS information and a free sample newsletter, write: COSMIC Awareness Communications, P O Box 115, Olympia, Washington 98507, USA)

MORE ON THE PHOTON BELT

This Awareness indicates that this so-called entry into the Photon Belt will nullify polarities for a short period of time which causes light to diminish and which will last for approximately less than a week—when it occurs, it will be relatively sudden. It is not as though there will be two months warning or six months from the time it occurs that people will witness this or that. It will occur suddenly; that light will tend to change and things will grow dark for a period of time, and the atmosphere will be much cooler during that dark period of time.

This Awareness indicates that the authors of the book **You Are Becoming A Galactic Human** describe in the book the probable sequence of events. Those event sequences are of less importance than the effects on consciousness itself, for entities will be experiencing certain changes in consciousness that will assist them in accepting what is happening in the environment. The photon energies, when coming in contact with earth, will have an effect on consciousness to give entities more of that which is likened unto "psychic powers." They will be able to sense that which they cannot see, to communicate psychically. Even though the telephone are not working and that electricity is not functioning, they will know what is occurring because the photon energy mingles with the energies of consciousness in such a way as to help carry information.

This Awareness indicates that the dimension you presently experience allows you to have access to the 49th octave of light; that which is the seven colors of the spectrum. When entering into the higher frequencies you will have other vibrations of light available to you in addition to the seven colors of light that make up the 49th octave. It is not so much that you will be in another octave, it is more that other octaves of lights will be made available; you will have additional perception into other dimensions without being totally yanked out of this dimension.

This Awareness is speaking of light colors and not of pigment colors. The light colors are vibrations or frequencies. These different frequencies tend to activate the chakras according to their sympathetic vibration to the chakras, and when you enter into the higher dimensional frequencies the chakras will be able to vibrate harmonically and sympathetically with the frequencies from higher dimensional colors and vibrations. Thus you will have an enhanced or increased type of awareness. Your consciousness will alter into higher frequencies and higher perception. You will appear to be more knowledgeable, more psychic, more sensitive and more aware. (From a September 6, 1995 reading).

Bibliography

All the books in this Bibliography have been reviewed by this author. The recommended reading are preceded by an asterisk.

French Books

Jaubert, Étienne, **Éclaircissement des Veritables Quatrains de Maitre Michel Nostradamus,** Amsterdame 1656.

Les Vrayes Centuries et Propheties de Maistre Michel Nostradamus, Amsterdame 1668.

Jant, Jacques de, **Predictions Tires des Centuries de Nostradamus,** Rouen? 1673.

Bareste, Eugène, **Nostradamus** second edition, Éditeur Maillet, Paris 1840.

Les Prophéties de Nostradamus, a Troyes, par Pierre Chevillot, Paris, Delarue, Libraire-Éduteur 1866.

Torne-Chavigny, H., **Portraits Prophétique d'Après Nostradamus,** Nantes 1871.

Larmor, Me Colin de, **Les Merveilleux Quatrains de Nostradamus,** Nates 1925.

*Fontbrune, Dr de, **Les Prophéties de Nostradamus Devoilées,** Éditions Adyar 1937.

*Fontbrune, Dr de, **Les Prophéties de Maistre Michel Nostradamus,** Michelet Éditeur, Sarlat 1939.

*Fontbrune, Dr de, **L'Etrange XXe Siècle Vue Par Nostradamus,** Michelet Éditeur, Sarlat 1950.

*Ruir, Emille, **Le Grand Garnage,** Éditions Médicis, Paris 1938.

*Ruir, Emille, **L'Écroulement de l'Europe d'Aprés les Prophéties de Nostradamus,** Éditions Médicis, Paris 1939.

*Ruir, Emille, **Nostradamus, Ses Prophéties de Nos Jours à L'an 2023,** Editions Médicis 1948.

*Ruir, Emille, **Nostradamus, Les Proches et Derniers Événements,** Éditions Médicis, Paris 1953.

Privat, Maurice, **La Fin de Notre Siècle et la Vie du Futur Grand Monarque d'Après Nostradamus,** Librairie Floury, Paris 1939.

Le Sort de L'Europe d'Après la Célebe Prophétie des Papes de Saint Malachie, P.V. Piobb, Editions Dangles, Paris 1939.

Les Propheties de M. Michel Nostradamus (Impreimee a Lyon par Benoift Riguard en L'An 1568), Imprenta de Biblioteca National, Buenos Aires 1943.

Nostradamus, Centuries Expliquees et Commentees, Editions de la Maison Française Inc., New York, 1944.

Alliaume, Maurice, **Magnus Rex de Nostradamus et Son Drapeau,** Published by the Author in France 1948.

Frontenac, Roger, **La Clef Secrète de Nostradamus,** Les Éditions Denoël, Paris, 1950.

Madeleine, George, **La Prochaine Gurerre Mondial Vue par Nostradamus,** Les Editions Provencia, Toulon, 1952.

Pichon, Jean-Charles, **Nostradamus et le Secret des Temps,** Les Productions de Paris 1959.

Pichon, Jean-Charles, **Nostradamus en Claire,** Robert Laffont, Paris, 1970.

Monterey, Jean, **Nostradamus Prophète du XXe Siècle,** La Nef de Paris Editions 1961.

Spanish Books

Krafft, Karl E, **Nostradamus Predice el Porvenir de Europa,** Ediciones Espanola, Madrid 1941.

Iveline, M.U., **Nostradamus,** Editorial Andiana, Buenos Aires 1967.

Garenciers, Theophilus de, **The True Prophecies or Prognostications of Michel Nostradamus, Translated and Commented,** London 1672.

*Robb, Steward, **Nostradamus on Napoleon, Hitler & the Present Crisis,** New York 1941.

*Robb, Steward, **Prophecies on World Events,** New York 1961.

Boswell, Rolfe, **Nostradamus Speaks,** New York 1941.

Lamont, Andre, **Nostradamus Sees All,** Philadelphia 1942.

*Leoni, Edgar, **Nostradamus: Life and Literature,** An Exposition-University Book, New York 1961.

Lavar, James, **Nostradamus, or the Future Foretold,** London 1942.

Allen, Hugh Anthony, **Window in Province,** Boston 1943.

Roberts, Henry C., **The Complete Prophecies of Nostradamus,** New York 1947.

Cheetham, Erika, **The Prophecies of Nostradamus,** A Perigee Book, New York 1973.

Cheetham, Erika, **The Further Prophecies of Nostradamus,** A Perigee Book, New York 1985.

Noorbergen, Rene, **Nostradamus Predicts the End of the World,** New York 1981.

Houghton-Brown, Geoffrey, **The Popes, Rome and the Church: According to the Oracles of Nostradamus, 1503-2055,** London 1981.

*Fontbrune, Jean-Charles, **Nostradamus Countdown to Apocalypse,** Henry Holt & Co., New York 1983.

Fontbrune, Jean-Charles, **Nostradamus 2, into the Twenty-First Century,** New York 1985.

*James Spike, **After 1984: the Secret Codes of Nostradamus Discovered,** Published by the Author, United States, 1984. This book includes an original reprint of: **Les oracles de Michel de Nostradamus by Anatole Le Pelletier.** Volume Two, Paris 1867.

Boyer, Nocodemus E., **Dr. M. Nostradamus: 1999, the Seventh Month,** Studeophile Publishers, Des Plaines, 111. 1985.

Pitt Francis, David, **Nostradamus: Prophecies of Present Times?** Aquarian Press 1985.

Hogue, John, **Nostradamus & the Millennium,** A Dolphin Book, 1991.

Hewitt, & Peter Lorie, **Nostradamus: The End of Millennium,** Simon & Schuster 1991.

*Cannon, Dolores, **Conversations with Nostradamus, 3 volumes,** Ozark Mountain Pub., Box 754, Huntsville, AR 72740, U.S.A., 1992.

Lorie, Peter, **Nostradamus, the Millennium and Beyond,** Simon & Schuster 1993.

*Ridge, Millie, **NOSTRADAMUS, An Illustrated Guide to his Predictions,** Smithmark, N.Y., 1993.

*Brennan, J.H., **NOSTRADAMUS: Visions of the Future,** Thorsons, 1992.

*King, Francis, **NOSTRADAMUS: Prophecies of the World's Greatest Seer,** St. Martin's Press, New York, 1994.

*Lemesurier, Peter, **NOSTRADAMUS: The Next 50 Years,** A Berkely Book, New York, 1994.

*Kidogo, Bardo, **The Keys to the Prediction of Nostradamus,** Foulsham, 1994.

Hogue, John, **NOSTRADAMUS: The New Revelations,** Element Books, 1994.

Video: ***The Prophecies of Nostradamus,** produced and directed by Paul Drane, American Video, 1979.

Video: ***The Man Who Saw Tomorrow,** produced and directed by Robert Guenette, Narrated by Orson Wells, David L. Wolper production, 1981.